OTHER TITLES OF INTEREST FROM ST. LUCIE PRESS

Inside ISO 14000: The Competitive Advantage of Environmental Management

ISO 9000: An Implementation Guide for Small to Mid-Sized Businesses

The 90-Day ISO Manual: Basics Manual and Implementation Guide

Competition in the 21st Century

The ISO 14000 EMS Audit Handbook

ISO 9000—The Blueprint (software)

QS-9000 Handbook: A Guide to Registration and Audit

Principles of Total Quality, 2nd Edition

Quality Improvement Handbook: Team Guide to Tools and Techniques

Total Quality Management: Text, Cases, and Readings, 2nd Edition

Introduction to Modern Statistical Quality Control and Management

Focused Quality: Managing for Results

Total Quality in Purchasing and Supplier Management

For more information about these titles call, fax or write:
St. Lucie Press
2000 Corporate Blvd., N.W.
Boca Raton, FL 33431-9868

TEL (561) 994-0555 • (800) 272-7737
FAX (800) 374-3401
E-MAIL information@slpress.com
WEB SITE http://www.slpress.com

S^t_L

Passing Your ISO 9000/ QS-9000 Audit

A Step-By-Step Guide

Donald A. Sanders, Ph.D.

S^tL

St. Lucie Press
Boca Raton, Florida

Copyright ©1997 by CRC Press LLC
St. Lucie Press is an imprint of CRC Press

ISBN 1-57444-128-0

Printed in the United States of America 10 9 8 7 6 5 4 3 2 1
Printed on acid-free paper

This book contains information obtained from authentic and highly regarded sources. Reprinted material is quoted with permission, and sources are indicated. A wide variety of references are listed. Reasonable efforts have been made to publish reliable data and information, but the author and the publisher cannot assume responsibility for the validity of all materials or for the consequences of their use.

Neither this book nor any part may be reproduced or transmitted in any form or by any means, electronic or mechanical, including photocopying, microfilming, and recording, or by any information storage or retrieval system, without prior permission in writing from the publisher.

All rights reserved. Authorization to photocopy items for internal or personal use, or the personal or internal use of specific clients, may be granted by CRC Press LLC, provided that $.50 per page photocopied is paid directly to Copyright Clearance Center, 27 Congress Street, Salem, MA 01970 USA. The fee code for users of the Transactional Reporting Service is ISBN 1-57444-128-0/97/$0.00/+$.50. The fee is subject to change without notice. For organizations that have been granted a photocopy license by the CCC, a separate system of payment has been arranged.

The consent of CRC Press does not extend to copying for general distribution, for promotion, for creating new works, or for resale. Specific permission must be obtained from CRC for such copying.

Direct all inquiries to CRC Press LLC, 2000 Corporate Blvd., N.W., Boca Raton, Florida 33431.

Table of Contents

Preface ix

About the Authors xiii

1 **The ISO Phenomenon** 1
   Learning Objectives 1
   Introduction 1
   What Is ISO 9000? 4
   History of ISO 9000 5
   ISO 9000 Requirements 7
   Evolution of the Audit Process 13
   ISO 9000 and the Service Industry 15
   The Audit Process 16
   Purpose of an Audit 22
   Recap 23

2 **Enter QS-9000** 25
   Learning Objectives 25
   Introduction 25
   Comparing ISO 9000 and Total Quality Management 26
   Moving Forward: The Quality Requirements of the Big Three 28
   Integrating ISO and CQI 30
   How QS-9000 Is Organized—An Overview 30
   What Are Sanction Interpretations? 33
   What Is the QSA? 33
   Developing a Checklist for the QS-9000 Audit 39
   Preparing for the QS-9000 Audit 40
   Recap 40

3 Preparing for the ISO/QS-9000 Audit: Planning the Implementation 43
Learning Objectives 43
Introduction 44
Initial Preparations 45
Deciding Upon Registration 58
Recap 62

4 Preparing for the ISO/QS-9000 Audit: Putting the Plan into Action 65
Learning Objectives 65
Introduction 65
Creating the Quality Manual and Documentation System 66
Contents of the Quality Manual 70
Standardizing and Writing SOPs and JWIs 82
The Pre-Audit 89
The Registration Audit 89
Recap 91

5 Selecting a Registration Firm 93
Learning Objectives 93
Introduction 93
The Confusion Over Registration 94
Criteria for Selecting a Registrar 96
Auditor Qualifications 115
Recap 118

6 The Internal Audit 119
Learning Objectives 119
Introduction 119
Planning Internal Audits 120
Preparing for an Audit 126
The Initial Meeting 135
Performing the Audit 137
Corroboration and Conclusions 145
The Final Meeting 146
The Final Report 148
Recap 150

7 The Registration Audit 151
Learning Objectives 151
Introduction 151
Be Auditor Friendly 152
The Pre-Audit Meeting 162
The Registration Audit 165

Final Meeting   182
   The Final Report   184
   Corrective Action   185
   Closeout Actions   188
   Recap   190
8 Summary 191
Bibliography 195

Preface

In the fall of 1987, an obscure set of standards, largely patterned after a set of British national requirements called BS 5750, is published by the International Organization for Standardization. Nine years later, the United States achieves its ten-thousandth registration to this now well-known phenomenon called ISO 9000 and worldwide registration surpasses 130,000! More than 7,000 suppliers of Chrysler and General Motors have been told that they must achieve registration to a companion called QS-9000, and several thousand Tier 2 firms have been put on notice that they must achieve "compliance" to this standard, with another 15,000 likely to follow.

I began consulting in ISO 9000 in 1991 as a result of a request by a client with whom I was working in the area of continuous quality improvement. This client was being required by a European customer to achieve ISO registration. At first, I found the language of the requirements baffling; the requirements themselves were inspection rather than improvement focused. But as time went on, it became apparent that my thinking and my paradigms about continuous improvement strategies were obscuring the potential of ISO, and later QS-9000. Today, I have a different view.

I would like to present an unusual paradigm for achieving ISO/QS-9000 registration. Instead of viewing the ISO/QS process as an externally imposed set of requirements which your company must satisfy through an unknown auditor, change the lens in the camera. Try to view the ISO/QS implementation process as a contest (or a game). The offense is represented by the forces for change, the forces focused on dramatically improving customer service, removing errors from the system, and structuring processes so that they ensure consistent improvement of product and service.

The defense is not the registrar; the registrar is more like a referee or an umpire, the one who assures that the game is played according to the rules. The rules are found in the standards themselves, which in turn can best be understood through the ISO guidelines and QS-9000-sanctioned interpretations.

The defense is really those in the company who don't want to change, who view ISO or QS-9000 as "a bureaucracy of paperwork" and a "creativity-stifling procedural nightmare." (Admittedly, both of these descriptions can be accurate if ISO/QS are not properly implemented; one company I visited had over 6,000 procedures!)

And victory? Winning the game is not simply achieving registration. It is seeing the small wins and the cost savings that come when errors are procedurally removed from a system. Victory is the absence of errors and an increase in business. It is personified in management involvement and continuous improvement of the system. Victory is in seeing and implementing ISO and QS-9000 as value-added tools rather than a set of rules and regulations for the quality department.

This leads us to the most prevalent myth about ISO/QS-9000—that they are quality standards. They are not. They are management systems, systems that begin by specifying the requirements for management in assuring the overall integrity of the quality process within a company. For that reason, winning this contest depends on the active involvement of management in assuring that the system is fully implemented and that it is regularly reviewed for improvement.

Too often, especially in big companies, ISO and QS are delegated to the quality department, when in reality, senior management must know not only what ISO/QS represents as a standard, but the inherent opportunity to improve processes and customer service that are woven throughout the requirements.

This book is based on experience with over 100 companies over the past nine years. It is designed as a blueprint for those wanting or required to achieve registration or compliance.

Chapter 1 begins with an introduction to the ISO phenomenon, as represented by the growth in ISO registrations from fewer than 100 in 1991 to over 10,000 by 1996. The chapter provides thorough coverage of the basics of ISO, including the differences between ISO 9001, 9002, 9003, and 9004. It also includes an introduction to the ISO audit process and provides the reader with insight into the "thinking of the auditor" during the registration audit.

Preface xi

While ISO 9000 is well known today, QS-9000 is less well known but growing exponentially in terms of registration activity and registrations. Chapter 2 provides an overview of QS-9000 and describes the similarities and differences between the ISO and QS systems. It points out the three critical references needed in order to pass the QS-9000 audit and provides an overview of how to achieve compliance to the four sections of the QS-9000 standard.

Chapter 3 begins the actual process of planning to achieve ISO or QS registration. It provides a step-by-step methodology which, if followed, will establish a companywide foundation to achieve ISO/QS registration.

Planning, of course, is followed by implementation, and Chapter 4 details specific steps that a company must take in terms of implementation. Beginning with determining which procedures need to be written and ending with receiving registration or achieving internal compliance, this chapter shows how you can develop and implement an auditable quality system.

Once your system has been implemented, the most important step in the process is the internal audit. Chapter 6 details a strategy for establishing an audit procedure and conducting internal audits. Key to this process is the development of comprehensive checklists. In QS-9000, some of the checklist questions are provided for you; for ISO 9000, a company must develop all its own. A key point is that if your system meets the requirements of the standard (ISO or QS), a thorough internal audit with comprehensive, targeted checklists should dramatically reduce the opportunity for nonconformances in the external audit. If your company wants to assure compliance to ISO or QS-9000, this is the culminating step in the process and should be celebrated internally as if you had actually achieved registration.

The culminating activity in the registration process is, of course, the external audit by the registrar. Chapter 7 shows you how to prepare for the audit, in particular how to prepare employees for the do's and don'ts of the audit itself (including "Ten Hints for Preparing for the Audit). This chapter also includes a list of those things that most auditors are trained to look for in assuring effective implementation of the requirements.

A word on compliance. In August 1996, several thousand tooling and equipment suppliers received notice of a new document, "Quality System Requirements—Tooling and Equipment Supplement" from the Big Three. Taking note of the tremendous strain that QS-9000 registration is putting on registration resources and not wanting to take resources away from the primary objective of registering Tier 1 suppliers, the Big Three noted that the Quality System Requirements and Tooling and Equipment Supplement should be seen as voluntary but "compliance is strongly recommended." Compliance is essentially everything in this book on ISO 9000 except selecting an auditor and holding the external audit. In pursuing compliance, always remember the first rule: "Without internal audit and management review, there is no compliance." For many tooling and equipment suppliers that want to be aggressive based on the notion that what is voluntary today may be required tomorrow, the first goal should be to achieve ISO 9000 registration in a manner that allows the company to meet the requirements of the Tooling Equipment Supplement and to have that fact noted by an external auditor on the audit report.

The goal of this book is simple. It is designed to help any company achieve registration or internal compliance to ISO/QS 9000. Using the book as a guide, the ISO/QS champion should be able to effectively prepare his or her company to achieve ISO or QS-9000 registration if required and compliance if not.

About the Authors

Dr. Don Sanders, president of Houston-based Sagent Consulting (formerly Total Quality Solutions), has been a consultant in Total Quality Management and ISO 9000 since 1986. His ISO 9000 consulting began in 1991, and he is proud of the fact that two of the companies that he consulted with were among the first 300 companies registered in the United States. He has specialized in applying the principles of ISO to companies in "nontraditional" industries (e.g., distribution, transportation, professional contract labor). His approach to ISO/QS-9000 registration as detailed in this book is practical, common sense, and based on his experiences working directly with more than thirty companies and indirectly (training, speaking) with hundreds more. Each company with with he has consulted has achieved the coveted "Recommendation for Registration" during the initial audit.

C. Frank Scott has designed and developed instructional training materials and simulations used by companies pursuing ISO registration. He has also been instrumental in developing several of the checklists as well as the ISO policy and procedures examples that are included in this book. He has presented training on the implementation of ISO 9000 and has worked with several companies in implementing the ISO 9000 process.

Chapter 1

The ISO Phenomenon

Learning Objectives

By the end of this chapter, you should be able to:

- Give two reasons for the explosive growth of ISO 9000* in the United States and throughout the world
- Explain how service companies fit into the ISO 9000 requirements
- Differentiate between an audit and an inspection, surveillance, or efficiency review
- Explain the differences between first-party, second-party, and third-party audits

Introduction

The impact of ISO 9000 registration on companies in the United States and around the world is staggering. Approximately 100 U.S. companies had achieved ISO registration by the end of 1991. By the end of 1992, the number of registered companies had grown to over 500. The numbers began to grow exponentially, and by mid-1996, the total was over

---

* ISO 9000 is referred to throughout this book. Because the ISO 9000 series is included in the QS-9000 standard, and because the continued use of the phrase ISO/QS-9000 is somewhat awkward, the phrase ISO 9000 is often used alone but in most cases is inclusive of QS-9000.

10,000 and still climbing. Many major auditing firms are adding two or three lead auditors per month to keep up with demand for ISO registration.

The drive for ISO registration by firms across the United States shows no sign of abating. A significant part of this growth is due to the fact that as companies complete their ISO registration process, it is not unusual for them to suggest to their major suppliers that they, too, become registered. A key provision of ISO 9001, Clause 4.6.2, has contributed to this phenomenon. It requires that companies assure the integrity of the vendor-approval process. One of the most effective ways to comply with this clause is to work with vendors that are certified to a recognized quality assurance standard, such as ISO 9000. This process has been fueled further by implementation of ISO-inclusive requirements such as QS-9000.

Of course, this phenomenon is not limited to the United States. The ISO 9000 series is now accepted as a quality standard in over 90 countries, essentially most of the industrialized nations and many developing countries. More than 15,000 companies in the United Kingdom currently are registered to one of the three ISO 9000 standards, and ISO's growth in Canada (where the standard is called Q 9000 and includes registration under Z299.0-.4) in many ways parallels that of the United States. The ISO 9000 series recently has gained greater impetus in the Pacific Rim area, particularly Japan. Today, over 130,000 companies are registered to ISO 9000 worldwide. (Some of the countries that have adopted the ISO 9000 standards are identified in Table 1.1.)

As a result of this activity, and the snowball effect of manufacturers requiring ISO registration of suppliers (which then require registration of *their* suppliers—the chains sometimes go six or seven companies deep), ISO 9000 registration is becoming more and more a requirement not only for doing business in Europe but for doing business worldwide.

Additionally, ISO 9000 is evolving from a standard originally thought to pertain only to manufacturing companies to one embraced by the service industry, software developers, the transportation industry, and wholesalers and distributors. Evidence of ISO 9000's shift from primarily a manufacturing standard to one that encompasses manufacturing, service, wholesaling, and distribution is seen in recent reports of registrations published by Quality Systems Update in its *ISO 9000 Registered Company Directory*. This directory, which has grown from 200 pages in 1990 to over 1,300 pages in 1996, shows tremendous growth in registration among those Standard Industrial Classification (SIC) codes dealing with service industries, such as 7300 (Business Services) and 5000 (Wholesale Trade-Durable Goods).

Table 1.1 Adaptation of Quality Standards Worldwide

Government or Other Body	Quality Management and Quality Assurance Standards: Guidelines for Selection and Use	Quality Systems: Model for Quality Assurance in Design/Development, Production, Installation, and Servicing
ISO	ISO 9000: 1987	ISO 9001:
Australia	AS 3900	AS 3901
Austria	OE NORM-PREN 29000	OE NORM-PREN 29001
Belgium	NBN X 50-002-1	NBN X 50-003
Canada	—	—
China	GB/T 10300.1-88	GB/T 10300.2-88
Commonwealth of Independent States	—	40.9001-88
Denmark	DS/EN 29000	DS/EN 29001
European Community	EN 29000	EN 29001
Finland	SFS-ISO 9000	SFS-ISO 9001
France	NF X 50-121	NF X 50-131
Germany	DIN ISO 9000	DIN ISO 9001
Hungary	MI 18990	MI 18991
India	IS: 10201 Part 2	IS: 10201 Part 4
Ireland	IS: 300 Part 0/ISO 9000	IS: 300 Part 1/ISO 9001
Italy	UNI/EN 29000	UNI/EN 29001
Malaysia	—	MS 985/ISO 9001
Netherlands	NEN-ISO 9000	NEN-ISO 9001
New Zealand	NZS 5600: Part 1	NZS 5601:
Norway	NS-EN 29000	NS-EN 29001
South Africa	SABS 0157: Part 0	SABS 0157: Part II
Spain	UNE 66 900	UNE 66 901
Sweden	SS-ISO 9000	SN-ISO 9001
Switzerland	SN-ISO 9000	SN-ISO 9001
Tunisia	NT 110.18	NT 100.19
United Kingdom	BS 5750: Part 0: Section 0.1 ISO 9000/EN 29000	BS 5750: Part 1: ISO 9001/EN 29001
United States	ANSI/ASQC Q 9000	ANSI/ASQC Q 9001
Yugoslavia	JUS A.K. 1.010	JUS A.K. 1.012

There is little doubt, then, that ISO registration for many companies has become a targeted activity. By the end of 1998, it is expected as many as 20 percent of U.S. companies with 25 or more employees will have achieved ISO registration. One firm that tracks ISO registrations in the United States estimates that as many as one-third of all nonretail U.S. companies will be registered to ISO 9000 by the end of the century.

What is ISO and how did it achieve such prominence so quickly? Before we examine the audit and registration process, let us first review briefly the what, why, and how of ISO 9000, because understanding the intent of ISO 9000 is really the first step in that long process toward passing the audit.

What Is ISO 9000?

ISO 9000 is a dynamic and comprehensive set of standards for a companywide quality system. The key words in this definition are *comprehensive* and *system*.

Comprehensive

ISO is comprehensive in that it goes beyond the realm of many quality certifications or standards that focus on production or the results of production (inspection data, for example). Instead, ISO looks at the primary variables that contribute to the overall ability of the product (or service) to meet the stated needs of the customer. For example, ISO 9001 was envisioned to include not only a significant section on process control but also a section related to how the company manages the quality of its purchasing function. ISO includes not only a clause (or section) related to how the company manages its storage, packaging, handling, and delivery but also one on how the company assures the customer that it can meet the requirements of the contract. Remember, ISO is not a quality standard, in a limited sense, but rather a management tool that impacts nearly everything a company does.

System

The second key word is *system*. In order to obtain ISO/QS registration, a company must document its overall quality system. ISO defines a quality system as the "organizational structure, procedures, processes and resources needed to implement quality management" (ISO 8402-1994:E 3.6). In other words, a quality system is the totality of practices that the company has developed, documented, and implemented to manage the delivery of a product or service that meets the requirements of the customer.

Although ISO 9000 has requirements for inspection and testing, its requirements go far beyond that. ISO 9000 is a standard for quality management and quality assurance; it is not simply an inspection process to eliminate any parts or services that do not meet a specific set of requirements. Under ISO 9000, quality is "built in," not "inspected in."

Think About It...

What type of quality system exists in your company? Does your company have quality by inspection or by process?

History of ISO 9000

The ISO 9000 standards have their origins in both Europe and the United States. ISO 9001, 9002, and 9003 share a common background with such standards as MIL-Q-9858 and NATO AQAP1, and, of course, they share significant commonality with the British Standards Institute series of standards—BS 5750, Parts 1, 2, and 3. Quality professionals involved in quality control and quality assurance probably are familiar with previous ISO standards issued by the International Organization for Standardization in Geneva, Switzerland.

The International Organization for Standardization

The International Organization for Standardization was founded shortly after the end of World War II to bring commonality and uniformity to products as well as to a number of critical quality areas. Over the past 50 years, the organization has issued more than 8,000 standards and technical reports and published more than 65,000 pages of technical text. Most Americans associate ISO with the 9000 series, but the 9000 series is only a very small part of ISO.

Development of the ISO 9000 series was a natural step for the International Organization for Standardization. As its other standards brought uniformity to products throughout Europe and the world, so the ISO 9000 series was designed to bring uniformity to the area of quality systems. Quality standards had proliferated as quality became more important to consumers and as each country—and often each industry—instituted its own quality standards. This large number of standards posed a hardship for many companies as they tried to keep track of the wide range of requirements and regulations. Multinational firms found it particularly difficult because they often had to juggle a number of often-conflicting regulations or face the fact that they might not be able to sell products designed for one country in another nation because they did not meet that country's unique standards. It was also becoming obvious that quality products and services demanded companywide commitment instead of just the efforts of the quality department.

Development of the Standards

The ISO 9000 series standards that we know today were developed by committees of quality experts selected from member bodies around the world. These members began meeting in 1979 as Technical Committee 176. The ISO member body in the United States is the American National Standards Institute, which has worked through the American Society for Quality Control to contribute to the development and ongoing improvement of the standards. Their work is accomplished through the efforts of individuals who are assigned to the working level of standards development and revision, the Technical Advisory Group.

When ISO develops a new set of standards, the initial series of standards is issued as a draft international standard, reviewed by representatives of the member bodies, revised, reviewed again, and finally issued as a complete standard. For example, ISO 9000-3, Guidelines for the application of ISO 9001 to the Development, Supply, and Maintenance of Software, originally was issued as a draft standard in 1990.

The process of revision is an integral part of the ISO process and, by implication, the QS-9000 process as well. The reason for this is inherent in the standards themselves—the concept of continuous improvement. Although standards always lag best practices, ISO is committed to narrow this gap as much as possible. The standards are revised and reissued about every five years. The first set of standards was published in 1987, and the first revision appeared in 1994. More extensive revisions are scheduled to be published around the year 2000. These revisions are expected to further extend ISO beyond the original manufacturing focus to service industries and software development and likely will be much more in alignment with the philosophy and precepts of continuous quality improvement and total quality management.

ISO does not stand for the International Organization for Standardization. ISO is taken from the Greek *isos,* meaning "equal," which is found in such common English words as *isosceles* (triangle), *isometric,* and *isonomy.* The International Organization for Standardization has three official languages—English, French, and Russian—and the acronym for the organization would be different in each language. "ISO" was chosen in an intentional effort to inform users that the standards apply to all users equally, regardless of a company's size, products, services, or the country in which it is located.

ISO 9000 Requirements

The ISO 9000 series asks a company to develop, document, and defend a series of quality management practices that range from management's responsibility for and commitment to quality (Section 4.1) to the quality management system used by the company (Section 4.2), from contract review (Section 4.3) and purchasing policies (Section 4.6) to inspection and testing procedures (Section 4.10), and from design review (Section 4.4) and statistical methods (Section 4.20) to training within the company (Section 4.18).

While each of the ISO 9000 standards addresses the entire spectrum of quality within a company, the standards vary in strictness. (A company involved in a comprehensive manufacturing process including design and installation has a greater number of issues to address than a company involved only in inspection and testing.) The standards, as of May 1997, are described briefly in the following sections.

ISO 9001

ISO 9001 (Model for Quality Assurance in Design, Development, Production, Installation and Servicing) is the standard of quality assurance for companies involved in all aspects of manufacturing, from design and development through production to installation and servicing of the product. Examples include major computer, automobile, or appliance companies as well as many suppliers to these companies which are involved in product design. ISO 9001 is function based, not size based (as are ISO 9002 and ISO 9003). Consequently, any company involved in processes ranging from the design of a product through the installation and service of that product should become registered to ISO 9001, whether the company has 2,000, 100, or 6 employees. ISO 9001 is addressed in 20 clauses and is the most comprehensive of the ISO standards. About 25 percent of the U.S. companies that have achieved ISO 9000 registration are registered to ISO 9001. As detailed in Chapter 2, ISO 9001 is the underpinning for the QS-9000 standard. (Table 1.2 gives a very brief description of the requirements of ISO 9001.)

Table 1.2 ISO 9001 Requirements

Clause 4.1 Management Responsibility
Clause 4.1 assigns top management the responsibility to define and document the quality policy and objectives for the organization, as well as to publicly state its own commitment to quality. Written forms, such as documents that can be exhibited in quality manuals, employee handbooks, required reading files, and bulletin boards, are acceptable, as are videotapes and personal presentations used in orientation training for new hires.

Top management must see to it that the responsibility, authority, and interrelationship of the people who manage, perform, or verify work that affects quality are defined. Each organization must determine for itself which activities do or do not affect quality, as defined by ISO 8402. Top management must periodically review the quality management system in order to satisfy the requirements of this standard. A management representative (one of the "supplier's management with executive responsibility") must be appointed to ensure the system is fully implemented.

Clause 4.2 Quality System
A documented quality system must be installed and maintained to ensure that the organization's products and/or services conform to specified requirements. In essence, the requirement is simply to develop a company-specific methodology to adequately address all of the other requirements of the standard; to then put this information into documented policies, quality plans, standard operating procedures, and work instructions; and to follow through with measures to put the system into operation, keep it current, and record its performance. Quality planning is a requirement.

Clause 4.3 Contract Review
This clause requires that procedures for contract reviews be established, maintained, and applied to each contract involving the organization. It also requires that records of these reviews be kept for future analysis. These contract reviews are to confirm that the customer's expectations are thoroughly defined and understood; that differences between the proposal and the contract are noted,; that the company is confident of its ability to meet or exceed those expectations; and that when changes occur, people who are impacted by the changes are notified.

Table 1.2 ISO 9001 Requirements (continued)

Clause 4.4 Design Control
The general purpose of this clause is to control and verify product designs to assure that they meet the requirements specified for them. This process includes detailing the duties associated with it, completely documenting requirements and designs, and subjecting the results of the process to a full review preliminary to gaining formal design approval.

A comprehensive design control process is fundamental to producing quality products and services. Such a process enables a company to effectively respond to customer expectations, safety considerations, technical standards, legal requirements, and manufacturing technology and/or capacity concerns very early in the life cycle of the product.

Clause 4.5 Document and Data Control
A company must establish and maintain methods for managing and controlling all documents and data that relate to quality. Any documents or data files relating to the quality system must be reviewed and approved for accuracy and adequacy before they are issued for general use. The document control system must incorporate methods to assure that current documents and data files are readily available at all work locations where they are needed. The quality system must include procedures for promptly and effectively removing obsolete records from distribution and/or storage. Changes or modifications to existing documents or data must be reviewed and approved by the same authority that approved the original material. There must be some method of fully identifying the current state or revision of "active" documents to preclude obsolete documents from being used.

Clause 4.6 Purchasing
This clause provides a structured safeguard to assure that everything purchased by a company conforms to specified requirements driven by the final application of the purchased materials. Written purchase orders must clearly describe the product being procured.

Clause 4.7 Control of Customer-Supplied Product
This clause requires a company to establish procedures to protect and maintain material supplied by a customer for use in a product that will be returned to that customer.

Clause 4.8 Product Identification and Traceability
A company must establish and maintain procedures that allow it to accurately identify its products from applicable design drawings, specifications, or other documents in appropriate situations during any stage of production, delivery, or installation. The means chosen to identify products must be sufficient to prevent confusion and inaccuracy. Another factor is the extent to which the ability to trace a product back to its origins is required or desired.

Table 1.2 ISO 9001 Requirements (continued)

Clause 4.9 Process Control
This clause requires that a company control all processes *that directly affect quality,* as defined in ISO 8402. This frequently includes many nonmanufacturing operations. A company must plan or identify its processes that directly affect quality and then ensure that those processes are carried out under "controlled conditions." These conditions include documented work instructions, sufficient equipment for the task, a suitable working environment, quality plans, a method for monitoring and controlling important characteristics of the product, the use of approved processes, and standards for quality of workmanship. A key change to this clause in 1994 was from requiring procedures for processes where their absence "would" adversely affect quality to "could" adversely affect quality.

Clause 4.10 Inspection and Testing
This clause requires management to define inspection and test levels appropriate to inspire customer confidence in a product's acceptability. The details of how this confidence is to be earned are usually described in documented procedures that spell out the methods and acceptance criteria and that tell what should be done when nonconformities occur. The amount and nature of receiving inspection and testing may depend on the supplier's proven quality record. Process inspections, tests, and product identifications must be done in a way that satisfies the quality plan or documented procedures. Process monitoring and control methods must be used to confirm that intermediate products conform to the requirements.

Clause 4.11 Control of Inspection, Measuring, and Test Equipment (IMTE)
The company must control, calibrate, and maintain IMTE so that it can demonstrate the conformance of its products to requirements. Companies must determine the appropriate level of accuracy for all measurements and use appropriate equipment, set calibration standards (including frequency) and document compliance with those standards, show calibration status of and maintain calibration records for IMTE, conduct calibrations in suitable environmental conditions, and calibrate the calibration instruments at specified intervals.

Clause 4.12 Inspection and Test Status
This clause requires that all products be identified by any suitable means that show whether or not a product has passed all required inspections and tests. These means include markings, authorized stamps, tags, labels, routing cards, inspection records, test software, physical location of the product, and so on.

Clause 4.13 Control of Nonconforming Product
A company must establish and maintain procedures to ensure that any product that does not conform to specified requirements is not used, installed, or mixed with conforming product. Procedures must be provided for identifying, documenting, evaluating, segregating, and disposing of nonconforming product. Nonconforming product may be reworked to meet requirements, accepted by the customer as is (with appropriate documentation), regraded for other uses, or scrapped.

Table 1.2   ISO 9001 Requirements (continued)

Clause 4.14 Corrective and Preventive Action
Companies must establish prevention-based systems that assure corrective action when defects are found. These corrective measures should be implemented, and revisions should be made to procedures and work instructions. This clause essentially requires a company to have implemented an effective customer complaint system.

Clause 4.15 Handling, Storage, Packaging, Preservation, and Delivery
The company must provide methods and means of handling products that prevent damage or deterioration. The company must provide secure storage areas or stockrooms to prevent the product from being damaged or from deteriorating prior to its delivery or use. Depending on the type of product, protection should be provided against water damage, temperature extremes, infestation by pests, corrosion, or contamination. If the product has a limited shelf life, there should be formal procedures to ensure that stock rotation is adequate to maintain the quality of the product. The company must control packing, preservation, and marking processes (including the materials used) to the extent necessary to ensure that the packaged product continues to conform to requirements specified for it.

Clause 4.16 Control of Quality Records
This clause requires that a company establish and maintain procedures to identify, collect, index, access, file, store, maintain, and dispose of quality records. Those procedures may be part of the overall organization's information management system or can be a distinct system that is part of the structure of the overall quality system. Quality records must be stored and maintained in a way that allows them to be readily retrieved. Storage facilities must provide a suitable environment to minimize deterioration or damage and prevent loss. Retention times of quality records must be established and recorded. Quality records must demonstrate that the required product quality and the effective operation of the quality system have been achieved.

Clause 4.17 Internal Quality Audits
A company must conduct internal quality audits, follow documented procedures during the audits and any follow-up actions, and must prepare and maintain an audit plan and records of the results. Audit findings should be based on objective evidence. Persons conducting the internal audits should be independent of the functions being audited. Results of internal audits must be documented and brought to the attention of those people responsible for the areas audited. The management personnel over those areas must take timely corrective action on any deficiencies found by an audit.

Clause 4.18 Training
A company must establish and maintain procedures for identifying training needs and then provide training for all people who perform activities that affect quality. People who perform tasks that involve specialized skills or specific assignments must be qualified for those tasks. One possible means of linking job assignments to training requirements is to incorporate those provisions into appropriate job descriptions, job assignment letters, notices, etc.

Table 1.2 ISO 9001 Requirements (continued)

Clause 4.19 Servicing
Where servicing is specified in a contract, the company must establish and maintain procedures for performing service and for verifying that it meets the specified requirements. Normally, service will include customer support at the company's facilities and in the field.

Clause 4.20 Statistical Techniques
Where appropriate, a company must establish procedures to identify adequate statistical techniques that verify the acceptability of process capability and product characteristics. The earlier a company institutes a comprehensive quality program based on statistical process control, the easier it will be for the company to support the growing importance of this clause.

ISO 9002

ISO 9002 (Model for Quality Assurance in Production, Installation and Servicing) is the standard for quality assurance for companies involved in production, particularly when multiple processes or an extended single process is involved, and for most service companies. Examples of companies that might require registration to this standard would be a tube manufacturer which begins with steel billets and produces pipe; a commodity chemical manufacturer with no research and design function; and almost any service company, particularly one in shipping, packing, distribution, wholesaling, or transportation. This standard is addressed in 19 clauses, an increase of one (servicing) from the 1987 standard. All changes made to ISO 9001 in 1994 apply word for word to ISO 9002. ISO 9002 does not address design. About 75 percent of U.S. companies registered to ISO 9000 are registered to 9002.

ISO 9003

ISO 9003 (Model for Quality Assurance in Final Inspection and Test) is the standard for quality assurance for companies involved in inspection or testing, companies with relatively simple and straightforward manufacturing processes, and companies that simply want to reassure their customers that they are providing quality assurance within their processes. This standard might be appropriate for companies that provide testing facilities; some heat-treating operations; companies with single-process manufacturing; and companies that provide a very simple service, such as accumulation and distribution (but not processing) of data. This standard is addressed in 16 clauses, with four "placeholders" inserted to allow consistency within the numbering system. The 1994 revisions to ISO added four new requirements to 9003: contract review, control of customer-supplied products, corrective action, and internal audits. Very few U.S. companies (less than 1 percent) are registered to ISO 9003. Frankly, since the changes included in the 1994 standard were published, there is very little benefit attached to registration to ISO 9003 compared to registration to ISO 9002.

ISO 9004

Many people confuse ISO 9004 with ISO 9001, 9002, and 9003. ISO 9004 differs from these standards in that it was not intended as a "checklist for compliance with a set of requirements" (ISO 9004-1987:E, p. 2). Instead, this standard establishes guidelines for the quality management philosophy and policies that should underpin registration to ISO 9001, 9002, or 9003.

ISO 9004 focuses on essential quality concepts such as defect prevention, customer focus, cost considerations, process control, documentation, purchasing, use of statistical evidence (control charts), training, and even motivation of employees. This standard should be read, understood, and implemented by all who wish to apply for ISO registration under 9001, 9002, or 9003.

Evolution of the Audit Process

The ISO 9000 standards were initially envisioned and implemented as a set of uniform audit criteria for second-party audits; that is, they were to be used by the customer in auditing its suppliers. While this was a major improvement in that suppliers could now comply with only one standard instead of the myriad used in the past, as the quality movement gained momentum it soon became apparent that the second-party audit system had some serious drawbacks. For example, if a company had 200 major suppliers, it would have to conduct 200 separate audits. Organizing these audits and employing people to conduct them would be an enormous—and expensive—task.

Suppliers faced a similar burden. If a supplier had 50 major customers, it would have to undergo 50 separate audits. Each audit would often take two days and sometimes even longer. The time and effort required to undergo and pass these audits were as big a burden to the supplier as conducting them was to the customer.

The process that exists today for ISO registration has evolved mainly because of the burden second-party audits placed on both the customer and the supplier. Third-party audits—audits conducted by independent registrars whose findings are acceptable to both the customer and the supplier—are today the hallmark of the ISO registration process. Although a customer could use the standards to audit its suppliers, it is rarely done. ISO registration by an independent registrar whose results can be communicated to a wide range of customers is instead the norm. "Killing two (or more) birds with one stone" is one reason why ISO registration has gained so much momentum since 1989. The 1994 revisions to ISO sanctioned this third-party registration process by expanding the scope of ISO 9001, 9002, and 9000 to include third-party certifications.

Think About It...

If your company had to be audited by each of its customers, how many audits would that entail? How long would it take? How long would it take your company to audit all its suppliers?

Internal Improvement

While most companies turn to ISO/QS-9000 as a means of reducing the number of audits they must undergo or because customers have made it a requirement for future business, others have adopted ISO for another reason: adherence to an ISO 9000 standard will enhance the internal operation of the company and thus make it more competitive.

A classic example of the use of the ISO 9000 series for internal improvement is Steelcase, Inc., a major manufacturer of office furniture with headquarters in Grand Rapids, Michigan, and 14 plants across the United States. Steelcase had no external pressure to adopt ISO 9000. It simply set a goal of achieving ISO 9001 registration at all 14 of its plants for the anticipated benefits of internal process control. So far, the results have been remarkable. Steelcase has encouraged its suppliers to achieve ISO registration, although it has not demanded registration. The more companies begin to perceive the benefits to be gained from registration, the more likely they will be to follow Steelcase's example.

ISO 9000 and the Service Industry

As the ISO registration process gains steam in the United States, the question of how nonmanufacturing suppliers fit in is becoming increasingly important. Every day, more and more people are asking, "What about service companies?"

As noted above, between 1987 and 1993, the major application of the ISO standards was in manufacturing. A review of the SIC codes for the more than 800 companies registered in the United States at the end of 1992 shows that more than 95 percent were in manufacturing of one kind or another. However, this situation is changing. Just as the move that began with manufacturing in the early 1980s from quality control to continuous quality improvement and total quality management evolved through to their service suppliers by the late 1980s, so is the ISO registration process beginning to have an impact on more and more companies that provide services to major manufacturing companies. Two years ago, interviews conducted with manufacturing companies about the need for their suppliers to achieve ISO registration often produced a response along the lines of "Let us first get our own house in order; then we'll worry about our suppliers." Today, however, similar questions prompt answers more along the lines of "We are trying to establish a fair and equitable time line for registration of our suppliers to an appropriate quality standard. With all the emphasis in ISO on approved suppliers, the most obvious way to assure a level of quality in all our suppliers, both manufacturing and service, is to require them to be registered by an independent organization to a quality assurance standard such as ISO 9002." Thus, a service company that supplies services to major manufacturing companies in the United States and/or Europe (e.g., an electrical distributor that supplies circuit breakers to a major computer manufacturer), or one that seeks the opportunity to work with these firms, will likely be affected by the ISO 9000 series in the very near future.

Including Service Companies in the Standards

The writers of the ISO standards were familiar with other quality standards in the United States and Europe (for example, MIL-Q-9858, NATO

NQAP1, and BS 5750). They also knew that quality audits, long a mainstay of such fields as medical products, chemicals, manufactured products, and products for the defense industry, were becoming more important in service and distribution. Thus, it is no surprise that the 1994 revisions were written with an eye toward including service firms.

The ISO authors achieved this by including in the revised ISO series definitions (ISO 8402-1994 E/F/R, Section 1.4—Terms and Definitions) a definition of a *product* as "the result of activities or processes" and *service* (1.5) as the "result generated by activities at the interface between the supplier and the customer and by supplier internal activities to meet the customer needs (such as the provision of a service or the execution of a production process)."

Think About It...

Is your company a service company? If so, which of the three standards (ISO 9001, 9002, or 9003) applies to your company? Why?

The Audit Process

Regardless of whether a company is a manufacturer or a service company, it is increasingly likely that ISO 9000 registration will be not just a competitive edge but a specific requirement for doing business with certain firms. In order to achieve ISO or QS-9000 registration, a company needs to understand one of the key elements of the registration process—the ISO/QS-9000 audit.

Companies seeking registration range from those very familiar with auditing process to those that have never been audited. Most major manufacturing companies, for example, have considerable familiarity with the auditing process. They frequently are audited by their customers or by outside auditing firms to assure compliance with standards such as MIL-Q-9858A, the Nuclear Regulatory Commission's 10CFR50, Specification Q-1 of the American Petroleum Institute, or the American Society of Mechanical Engineers' NQA-1, 1989. In addition, many of these companies may have been audited to a quality standard specific to a customer, such as the Ford Q-101 standard.

The Malcolm Baldrige National Quality Award also has increased the overall level of awareness of the auditing process for a number of U.S.

companies. Whether or not they have actually received a visit from a Baldrige examiner, many companies using the Baldrige criteria for quality improvement have conducted thorough internal audits of their customer service, leadership, human resources, planning, measurement, and information systems. (ISO 9000 [1994] addresses about half of the Baldrige criteria.)

At the other end of the continuum are companies for which the auditing process will be a new experience or for which the arrival of an auditor on site is a rarity. These firms include many smaller manufacturers or repair shops, many distributors and wholesalers, many service companies, and even some retailers. While most of these companies will have undergone a financial audit, very few will have had to meet a national standard for quality and may have received only the infrequent customer visit/audit.

What Is an Audit?

To most people, the first thing that comes to mind when they hear the word *audit* is a financial accounting. While that is where the term originated, "audit" has since evolved to include any type of systematic examination of a process. For the purposes of this book, an audit will be defined as *an independent, systematic, and documented activity to evaluate, verify, and report on—by means of the examination of objective evidence—compliance with the requirements of a quality specification or other standard.* A brief review of the elements of this definition will help clarify the overall rationale supporting the audit process.

Audits Are Independent Activities

First, an audit is an independent activity. There are three types of audits: first party (internal), second party, and third party.

First-Party (Internal) Audits

First-party or internal audits are, as the name implies, typically done by someone inside the company. The most common purpose of the internal quality audit is to assure the organization's top management that the quality system is performing up to expectations (one of the three objectives of a quality system outlined in ISO 9000). The internal auditor, although a member of the organization, typically is someone not officially responsible for routine duties involving the development or operation of the quality system. ISO 9001, 9002, and 9003 and QS-9000 require companies seeking registration to perform internal audits. In fact, ISO 9000 requires that an internal auditor be independent of the function being audited and that the results of the audit be reviewed by the company's highest level of management. (The internal audit process is discussed fully in Chapter 6.)

Second-Party Audits

Second-party audits are conducted by a member of a customer organization as a way to verify that the supplier's products and/or its quality system are adequate. This once was the main type of audit, but it is being superseded by third-party audits to standards like the ISO/QS-9000 series. However, second-party audits are still done, especially if a customer imposes more stringent requirements than those included in the ISO 9000 series. This practice is most common in specialized fields such as medical products. (Second-party audits follow the same basic procedures as third-party audits, but the criteria are often specialized.)

Third-Party Audits

Third-party audits are conducted by an external, independent auditing organization, usually to a recognized standard. Third-party audits can assess both products and systems. When conducted by organizations with nationally recognized accreditation, they can also be beneficial in areas such as:

- Helping to reduce the number of second-party audits required by customers
- Serving as a source of information to use in improving the operations of a supplier
- Providing the marketing advantage that comes with having a registered product or quality system
- Gaining access to markets that require quality system registration

In essence, ISO/QS-9000 audits are third-party audits that, when successfully completed, indicate to customers that the audited company has a system for quality assurance that is in place and functioning. (While the ISO [third-party] auditing process is discussed fully in Chapter 7, one caveat is important at this juncture: not all ISO 9000 registrars are QS-9000 registrars. More on this in Chapter 7.)

Think About It...

Has your company ever undergone an internal audit? A second-party audit? A third-party audit? How did they differ from one another?

Inherent in all three forms of audits is the concept that the people conducting the audits are independent of the activity being audited. ISO 9001 (1994), Section 4.17 echoes this commonly accepted criteria of the audit: "...quality audit...shall be carried out by personnel independent of those having direct responsibility for the work being audited." The independence of the auditors is generally not a problem when the audit is a third-party audit conducted by an outside auditing firm (e.g., DNV or Underwriters Laboratories) or a second-party audit conducted by quality auditors from a customer (e.g., General Motors or Hoechst Celanese). It can be an issue with internal audits, especially for smaller companies. Companies must take steps to ensure the independence of internal auditors.

Audits Are Systematic

The second important characteristic of an audit is that it is systematic. Audits are based on criteria that relate to a specification such as NQA-1 or ISO 9002. As such, the audit necessarily will include checklists to ensure compliance to the standard. The checklists, which are compiled before the audit begins, are used to assure that the audit activity itself has some inherent predictability and consistency, and that there is as little randomness and variation as possible, given the parameters of a specific audit. (Examples of these checklists are shown in Figures 6.1 and 6.2.) In other words, whether the audit is being conducted at a sophisticated manufacturer of silicon wafers or at a ten-person branch of an auto parts distributor, the auditors will verify by means of checklists or other established criteria that the system being audited meets the requirements of the standard.

Auditors are cautioned to rely on—but not to be bound by—the checklist or other criteria with which they begin the audit. In practice, this means that when a nonconformance is found, it will likely give rise to questions not on the audit checklist but that bear directly on whether or not the company being audited actually meets the intent of the standard. Most registrars regularly update their checklists both to assure compliance with the standard and to focus in on areas such as document control, where more nonconformances are being found.

Audits Are Documented Activities

The third element of an audit is that it is documented. The auditor begins the audit process with some sort of criteria checklist. The entity being audited is examined for compliance with the checklist. Records of the degree of compliance are maintained, nonconformance reports are written, discrepancies are noted, and an overall report of the audit is generated. All of this is documented. An audit without documentation, no matter how thorough, is merely a visit.

Objective Evidence

There is probably no more important term in the auditor's lexicon than *objective evidence*. Most auditors will rely on data that can be observed—seen, touched, or heard. They will want to examine records, search through files, visit the shop floor, and inspect the warehouse. If you tell an auditor that you have been keeping data on customer complaints for six months and have used them for corrective action for the last four months, the auditor will want to see proof of this.

Why the emphasis on objective evidence? Some of the reasons are obvious. For example, a company representative could claim that, in compliance with Section 4.13.1 of ISO 9001, the procedure for disposal of nonconforming material has been in place for a year. But if the auditor can find no evidence of this (records of the meetings of a materials review board, documents confirming that customers have been called regarding concessions on some products that do not meet specification, records of reworking material to meet specification, or an indication of how much product is scrapped after inspection), the claim is not likely to be valid.

Another reason for the emphasis on objective evidence is the potential for communication breakdown. A word or a phrase may have a different meaning to the auditor than it does to the company. For example, a company might consider brief, informal checks of various aspects of its operation "internal audits," whereas an auditor probably would not. Examination of objective evidence clears up much of this kind of confusion.

Yet another reason for the pursuit of objective evidence is related to the "halo effect." The halo effect occurs when an auditor feels that the auditee (the company or function being audited) can do nothing wrong. If, for example, all the answers are correct and all the data are available on the first day of the audit, the auditor begins to assume that the company is totally prepared, even if it is not. Objective evidence eliminates this subjective element and allows the auditor to gain a true picture of the system being audited.

Evaluate and Verify

The job of the auditor is to make an evaluation of the entity being audited in order to verify that it meets the intent of the standard. While auditors attempt to minimize variation in the audit process, every audit has some subjectivity inherent in the process. While the auditor relies on objective evidence, the auditor's personal experience, strengths, and skills will always be a part of any audit process. To minimize the impact of subjective judgment, not only is objective evidence sought, but specified criteria on the checklist are detailed so that the evaluation of a product or system is replicable, as much as possible, from one auditor to another.

Once the evidence is evaluated, it is important to verify its implementation within the company or department being audited. For example, an auditor may examine a written procedure to evaluate its compliance with ISO 9001, Section 4.11. The next step is to verify that this procedure is being implemented as stated. Verification takes the auditor into the area of real-world application of the procedure.

What an Audit Is Not

As important as knowing what constitutes an audit is knowing what an audit is not. First, an audit is not an inspection. It is not testing the pressure of a valve to see if it meets the specification and then pronouncing "go" or "no go." It is not merely checking a product, or a number of products, to ensure that they meet customer requirements. Passing a product inspection is not the same as passing a quality audit.

An audit is also not the same as ongoing surveillance, which in many quality standards is just "monitoring." (However, under ISO 9000/QS-9000, surveillance visits [periodic audits to ensure the quality system is maintained and running properly] are an integral part of the audit process.) An audit also is not a type of efficiency review or a cursory examination of a department to assure that it is profitable as a cost center.

Purpose of an Audit

Some may question why auditing is required at all. Why can't a company just send evidence of the success of its system (such as control charts) to an independent agency, have the agency review the evidence, and then have the agency pronounce the company a worthy vendor, a quality distributor, a verified manufacturer, etc.? This question really asks about the purpose of an audit.

At the heart of all audits are two concepts: compliance and improvement. Compliance means meeting a requirement or a series of requirements imposed by an outside source. It is a finite goal and is measured in "yes" or "no" terms; either a company is in compliance with the requirements imposed upon it or it is not. Improvement is making things (products, a process, a system) better; it is usually imposed by the company itself. It is an infinite goal and is measured in increments. A series of audits helps a company achieve both these goals. Once a company understands the dual purpose of an audit (compliance and improvement), its notion of the ISO audit changes.

Because the audit will often focus on meeting the spirit as well as the letter of ISO compliance, a company should assure two things before it requests an ISO/QS audit: it should be certain that the quality system works and it should build in proactive methods for improving service to the customer. Some auditors have said things like, "I look for evidence of a proactive, prevention-based system. If I find that, I may allow a little slack if some of the records are misplaced." When such auditors find a totally reactive system, one that is designed only to find errors after they happen and correct them, they tend to be far more stringent.

A proactive system also negates the concept of the auditor as a "spy" who is looking for things that do not meet the standard. A company with a proactive system, one that tries to ferret out potential errors before they occur, can share with the auditor the benefits of that system.

Recap

Registration to one of the ISO 9000 standards by U.S. companies has grown exponentially since 1989. More than 11,000 U.S. firms will be registered to one of the standards by mid-1996. Part of the reason for the boom is that the first wave of companies that became registered are now requiring their suppliers to become registered. Many companies in this second wave are service companies.

As companies implement ISO, they become involved in the audit process. Audits are systematic, documented examinations of every area of the company that affects quality (the quality system). They involve searches for documented evidence to show whether the company's quality system meets the intent of the ISO standards. A company should make its quality process proactive rather than reactive.

Chapter 2

Enter QS-9000

Learning Objectives

By the end of this chapter, you should be able to:

- Identify two major differences between ISO 9000 and QS-9000
- Explain the role of ISO 9000 within the QS-9000 system
- Identify who must qualify under the QS-9000 requirements
- Specify the purpose of "Sanctioned Interpretations"

Introduction

As ISO 9000 continued to grow in popularity, there was increasing concern among some quality professionals that "being ISO registered" would become synonymous with "having an outstanding quality process." Customers of many ISO-registered suppliers realized that it was not, that the ISO standards and the registration process were missing key ingredients of a total quality management (TQM) system, and that ISO often guaranteed consistent, but not ever-improving, quality. The late Dr. W. Edwards Deming, who brought quality concepts to the attention of many American leaders, particularly in the automotive industry, noted that ISO 9000 was simply another set of requirements meant to assure minimum levels of performance and that were not much better than the previous standards it replaced.

In addition, the Malcolm Baldrige National Quality Award (which saw interest decline in the Baldrige Award as interest in ISO increased) became concerned about the proliferation of a quality standard that recognized adherence to requirements rather than commitment to customers, employees, and continuous improvement. Whereas the Baldrige could be awarded to no more than six companies in any given year, there were more than 2,000 registrations to the ISO 9000 set of standards in 1993 alone. This fact by itself was enough to turn the attention of many companies away from the Baldrige Award and toward ISO. Add in the fact that ISO is typically achievable in 18 months or less and that it can be achieved based on meeting predetermined criteria rather than competitive performance, and ISO became the obvious choice for most American companies.

On top of that, beginning in about 1992, banners began going up on interstates and back roads all over the United States proclaiming, "XYZ Manufacturing—ISO 9001 Registered." Registered companies were putting little symbols on their stationery and business cards signifying that they were registered, and qualified registrars were growing in number, doubling every year for three years running.

All of this was causing confusion and alarm in some circles. Pressure, usually indirect, was being put on Ford, Chrysler, and General Motors to accept, in full or in part, ISO 9000 registration as evidence of a fully functioning quality system. Predictably, there was resistance from the automakers, based not on what was often called arrogance of size and "clout" but rather resistance related to what the Big Three had been trying to accomplish in terms of quality with their suppliers since the early to mid-1980s.

Comparing ISO 9000 and Total Quality Management

It is important to again note that quality standards always lag best practices. Remember that the concept of an international standard for quality had its beginnings only in 1979 and that the model for ISO 9000 was a European quality standard far removed from the philosophies of W. Edwards Deming, Joseph Juran, Armand Feigenbaum, or any other American quality "guru." As a matter of fact, the underlying structure for ISO was primarily based on a widely used standard in the United Kingdom—BS 5750—with requirements and/or language from other European, American, and NATO standards integrated into the process.

ISO as Minimum Requirements

In the early years of ISO registration, it was not uncommon to hear something like, "To become ISO registered you simply have to do three things: say what you do, do what you say, and prove it." While it was later added that all of this had to meet the requirements of ISO 9001, 9002, or 9003, this simple saying contained the seeds of the problems that ISO registration would present when it came up against a quality process based on the teachings of Juran or Deming. Critics asked, "Where is the equivalent of *cease dependence on mass inspection* in the ISO standards," as is required by Deming's second of his famous Fourteen Points. "Where is *drive out fear* or *continuously improve the methods of production?*" They are not a part of ISO, not even in the 1994 revisions, because ISO (the critics noted) is still focused more on inspection than improvement.

While in fairness it should be mentioned that some of these issues were, in fact, addressed in the revisions issued in 1994 (preventive action is certainly consistent with Deming's fifth point: *"Find problems—it is management's job to continually work to improve the system")*, ISO still remains, in the perception of those who are familiar with TQM and continuous quality improvement (CQI), a set of minimum requirements built around the old idea of inspections (incoming, in-process, and final), with little or no commitment to formalize the process of continuous improvement.

ISO 9000—Good Business Practices

Much of this minimizes the contribution that can be made by a fully implemented quality system in the ISO format. As has often been noted, developing and creating a quality system consistent with ISO is a good first step toward implementing a customer- (or market-) oriented quality improvement process. It is amazing how many companies in the United States (not just in service but also in manufacturing) function with no written procedures at all, or if they have written procedures, they are outdated, poorly written, rarely used, and certainly there is no documentation to suggest their full implementation.

For companies in this state of affairs—companies without formalized procedures, companies where training consists of passing down folk wisdom from the experienced to the inexperienced and thus perpetuating not only outdated processes but the mistakes inherent in these outdated processes—ISO can be quite a boon. Taking time out to develop, write, formalize, and implement processes in critical areas such as process control, purchasing, and contract review does improve the level of service provided to customers—even if it is not "world class."

Further, ISO does contain elements consistent with the philosophy of continuous improvement. The requirements for management review, quality planning, contract review (not promising what you cannot deliver), design control, purchasing (narrowing your supplier base using quality, not just price, as a basis), inspection, measuring and test equipment, preventive and corrective action, training, and use of statistical methods are all critical in the implementation of a fully functioning TQM process. But some are not consistent, and the paperwork involved in documenting the quality system can take time away from the important activities involved in continuously improving processes and focusing on the needs of the customer or marketplace.

Think About It...

What is the main criticism that has been leveled at ISO by the proponents of TQM and continuous improvement?

Moving Forward: The Quality Requirements of the Big Three

As part of a process of requiring higher and higher levels of performance from their suppliers of manufactured parts, tooling and equipment, and service, the three major U.S.-owned automotive companies (Ford, Chrysler, and General Motors) developed and implemented, complete with audits, their own quality standards. Ford had its *Q-101*, Chrysler its *Supplier Quality Assurance*, and General Motors its *Targets for Excellence* in North America and *General Quality Standard* in Europe. In addition, these standards were often customized to fit a specific industry—to the point where, for example, a version of Ford's Q-101 standard (Q-1) had been adapted to service companies that provided professional contract labor (accountants, engineers, information technology specialists). Additionally, there was significant variation within these systems which left some parts suppliers wondering what they needed to do to produce predictable levels of quality. By the early 1990s, as international competition took over more than 30 percent of the U.S. auto market, it was time for the paradigm of competition within standards to be replaced by cooperation within standards.

What Is QS-9000?

The cooperation that produced QS-9000 is a direct result of two related forces for the 1990s—internationalization and harmonization. Internationalization became more of an issue during the 1980s and 1990s. Obviously, as companies became global and international rather than local and national, the need for interchangeable parts and assemblies grew, and the need for consistency in these components became paramount. This is one of the advantages of a system like ISO; a customer can be assured of a relatively consistent product because all those who manufacture it anywhere in the world are following a similar set of procedures instead of simply trying to somehow meet a similar set of specifications.

Harmonization, on the other hand, is a fairly revolutionary concept in an industry traditionally dominated more by competition than cooperation. Harmonization is the agreement among Ford, GM, and Chrysler and some large tractor truck manufacturers (e.g., Freightline) to integrate their separate quality requirements into one unified document called QS-9000.

Thus, QS-9000 *is a cooperatively developed and administered standard that integrates ISO 9000 with continuous improvement requirements and manufacturing capabilities.* In understanding what QS-9000 is, it is important to remember that, like ISO 9000, QS-9000 is not just for the quality department. It is not a quality standard in the traditional sense, but rather a management system that begins with a management requirement. As with ISO, QS-9000 is broad based, requiring the involvement of a wide range of functions (e.g., sales, purchasing, executive, engineering, manufacturing, training) in securing registration.

History of QS-9000

The harmonization process that led to the development of QS-9000 really began in mid-1988 at a meeting of senior-level purchasing managers. The meeting was held under the auspices of the Automotive Division of the American Society for Quality Control. Out of this meeting came the initial cooperative venture—the Supplier Quality Requirements Task Force. In 1990, this team issued its first harmonized publication, a manual detailing a methodology for calibrating measurement devices and evaluating the amount of error present in such devices.

In 1992, a second manual, one dealing with statistical process control, was issued for distribution through the Automotive Industry Action Group (AIAG). Other manuals followed. At the same time, interest in ISO 9000 was growing dramatically, and a logical question was, "Why not use ISO as a basis for establishing a common system of requirements for all major U.S. automakers?"

During 1992 and 1993, draft documents were developed and circulated for review. In 1994, the document was issued as *Quality System Requirements: QS-9000,* and it was announced that QS-9000 would immediately replace previous quality requirements programs such as *Q-101* and *Targets for Excellence.* In the fall of 1994, the Big Three sent out over 15,000 letters to their Tier 1 suppliers, notifying them of the change and identifying the need to achieve third-party registration to QS-9000.

Integrating ISO and CQI

As the QS-9000 standard is read for understanding, the objective of the authors in integrating CQI and ISO 9000 becomes apparent. There is an entire section on continuous improvement, including a requirement for the deployment of a comprehensive philosophy of continuous improvement and a companywide commitment to continuously improving "quality, service (including timing, delivery) and price for all customers." There is also a section on customer-specific requirements which, for example, require that a company seeking registration for Ford follow the Quality Operating System (QOS) model. This QOS model is a direct descendent of the "Quality Is Job 1" Ford quality process/program. Following a brief overview of the structure of the QS-9000 document, each of the sections will be covered in greater detail.

How QS-9000 Is Organized—An Overview

QS-9000 integrates ISO 9001 into the automakers' requirements and adds additional sector- and customer-specific requirements. QS-9000 is organized into four sections:

- **Section 1: ISO 9000 Requirements**—This section includes the complete text of ISO 9001. Each element of the standard is identified as it is in the 1994 revisions to ISO 9001, Sections 4.1 to 4.20. The ISO requirements are in italic type. Following this italic text are the

additional requirements of the automotive/heavy truck manufacturers. These are in regular type.
- **Section 2: Sector Specific Requirements**—This section seems relatively minor in terms of space, but it is really the key difference between ISO and QS-9000 in that it mandates processes for continuous improvement, production and part approval, and manufacturing capability. Because automotive manufacturers have been requiring these processes from their parts suppliers for some time now, these requirements will not mean major changes for most suppliers, although they may mean additional documentation.
- **Section 3: Customer Specific Requirements**—These are the requirements that are unique to either Ford, General Motors, or Chrysler. Requirements for the heavy truck manufacturers are found in separate documents issued by each company. It is critical that you discuss with your customer which requirements pertain to current or future contracts. Tier 1 Chrysler suppliers are required to adopt these standards by July 31, 1997 and Tier 1 General Motors suppliers by December 31, 1997.
- **Section 4: Appendices**—The appendices can be very helpful for a company seeking QS-9000 registration. For example, Appendix A describes the registration process, and Appendix G includes requirements for registrars and auditors. Appendix H describes the minimum time that a registration visit will take based on size and complexity. If your company will be seeking QS-9000 registration, make sure that the ISO champion and/or management representative review the Appendices.

The Four Sections—The Integration of ISO and CQI

As noted earlier, QS-9000 integrates CQI and ISO 9000, thereby creating a standard that is both more comprehensive and more difficult to achieve. For example, in Section 1, Element 4.1 (Management Responsibility), not only are the ISO requirements for responsibility and authority, resources, management representative, and management review included, but there are also requirements for a comprehensive business plan (not subject to third-party audit), analysis and use of company-level data, and customer satisfaction. This requirement for determining levels of customer satisfaction (trends, key indicators, benchmarks, comparisons to competitors) is the first of many requirements that make QS-9000 resemble a hybrid of the Malcolm Baldrige National Quality Award and ISO 9000 rather than simply a more rigorous or industry-oriented version of the international standard. Whereas the text of the 20 ISO 9001 elements is included in 9 pages, the parallel QS-9000 requirements take more than 40 pages!

Section 2 (Sector Specific Requirements) only contains five pages of introduction and text, but because it mandates that the supplier comply with the Production Part Approval Process (PPAP) as described in the PPAP Manual, *and* develop action plans for continuous improvement of those areas deemed most important to the customer, *and* improve manufacturing capabilities, it will certainly require considerable effort to implement and document adherence to the requirements of Section 2. This section contains requirements for activities as diverse as "mistake-proofing," determining "cost of quality," monitoring processes through "variables and attributes control charts," using "benchmarking," and implementing improvement projects to reduce "excessive cycle time." As noted above, while none of this is likely new to those who have been supplying Ford, GM, and Chrysler since the mid-1980s, assuring that it is fully documented and accessible in an auditor-friendly system may require a system review and procedural changes.

Section 3 (Customer Specific Requirements) resembles a listing of requirements for good manufacturing practices from each of the three automakers and references publications with which most current parts suppliers are very familiar, including Chrysler's *Priority Parts Quality Review* and *Design Review Guidelines* and Ford's *Potential Failure Modes and Effects Analysis Handbook* and *Heat Treat System Survey Guidelines*. Unlike Ford and Chrysler, General Motors did not include any individual requirements in this section; however, GM does reference 15 publications that contain requirements which "shall be met by GM NAO (North American Operations) suppliers."

As noted in the overview, Section 4 (Appendices) is not to be overlooked when preparing for your company's QS-9000 audit. For example, Appendix B specifies that each time the registrar conducts an on-site audit, it shall include a review of customer complaints and the supplier's response to those complaints, internal audits and the supplier's response to those audits, and progress toward meeting continuous improvement targets. Appendix B also includes the requirement that the registrar's checklist shall include, but not be limited to, all the questions in the Quality System Assessment (QSA) (discussed later in this chapter). Further, if any open major *or minor* nonconformances (as defined in the QSA) exist against the items on the QSA, *registration shall not be granted* (italics added). This is far more rigorous than ISO registration, which will typically discover several minor nonconformances (up to 25 in some companies!) during the audit and still recommend registration. Be certain to check with your registrar as to the specific implementation of this requirement. This leads to one other significant difference between ISO and QS-9000: the use of "sanctioned interpretations."

What Are Sanctioned Interpretations?

One of the problems that companies new to the ISO process have typically experienced is that the language of ISO is open to interpretation. The administrators of the QS-9000 process were determined to avoid this as much as possible through the use of a group of "sanctioned interpretations." These interpretations are issued every few months by the International Automotive Sector Group and must be used by anyone desiring to achieve QS-9000 registration. The purpose of these interpretations is to clarify and resolve interpretation issues related to QS-9000. For example, one question covered in the March 22, 1996 issue is:

> "Do the PPAP requirements apply to temporary out source, plant assists or emergency run situations? What if you only have the job a weekend, a week, a month or a few months?"
>
> **Answer:** "Yes, you must notify your customer. These situations may be handled under 4.13.4 Engineering Approved Product Authorization, or by a PPAP submission, based upon the customer's direction."

Copies of these interpretations are available from the American Society for Quality Control (800-248-1946) or through the ASQC QS-9000 Web site (http://www.asqc.org/9000). They are also published in *Quality Systems Update*, which is published monthly by Irwin Professional Publishing. Because they are issued every few months, make sure that you check at least every three months for new interpretations.

What Is the QSA?

An additional document that is available through the AIAG is called the Quality System Assessment. It is one of the most important documents that a company can obtain in terms of passing the QS-9000 audit as it includes a checklist of questions which can help the company determine how well its processes are meeting the requirements of QS-9000. The importance of this document in preparing for and passing the audit cannot be overemphasized. The document is used to help train auditors for QS-9000, and it is frequently used by registrars to develop the actual generic checklists (those outside the company's unique procedures) that they use during audits. Between the QS-9000 document, the sanctioned interpretations, and the QSA (note that the QSA does not cover all of the requirements of QS-9000), a company seeking QS-9000 registration is essentially provided a detailed blueprint for registration. In this sense, QS-9000, even though it is a more rigorous management system standard than ISO (because of the addition of process capability, continuous improvement, and customer-specific requirements), can be more easily targeted and planned than ISO 9000.

Think About It...

What two documents represent a significant departure of QS-9000 from the ISO 9000 model?

Does QS-9000 Apply to Your Company?

There has been much confusion as to who is covered by the requirements of QS-9000, despite efforts to clarify the matter. Let's begin by looking at the requirement of the standard:

> QS-9000 applies to all internal and external suppliers of: a) production materials; b) production or service parts; or c) heat treating painting, plating or other finishing services directly to Chrysler, Ford, General Motors or other OEM customers subscribing to this document.

This seems to be fairly clear; it obviously applies to all Tier 1 suppliers of parts and services. However, in March 22, 1996 IASG Sanctioned QS-9000 Interpretations (9602-A25 Agreed-February 15, 1996), the requirement is extended to a supplier of a supplier; a warehouse/distribution company had been told by some registrars that the company did not qualify to become registered under QS-9000! The lesson here is that all Tier 1 suppliers to Ford, GM, or Chrysler should seek QS-9000 registration; companies with any other standing should check with their custom-

Enter QS-9000 35

ers—and keep checking back every four to six months. Because ISO 9000 requirements are essentially a subset of QS-9000 requirements, achieving QS-9000 registration conveys ISO 9001 or 9002 registration.

What Are the Differences Between an ISO and QS-9000 Audit?

One of the obvious differences between the two audits is that QS-9000 is more comprehensive than ISO. Not only does the QS-9000 standard require that a company comply with two additional sections in order to become registered, but the section based on ISO is more extensive. In fact, of the 20 requirements of ISO 9001, only Sections 4.3 (Contract Review), 4.8 (Product Identification and Traceability), and 4.19 (Servicing) are left unchanged.

QS-9000 registration requires that a company have a comprehensive philosophy of continuous improvement, with a systematic methodology for assuring implementation and evidence that this implementation is effective. In addition, QS-9000 expects that a company pursuing registration will use design and process FMEAs (failure modes and effects analysis), control charts, and process capability studies. More attention is given to the adequacy of resources and the storage and maintenance of tools.

Finally, as noted above, not all ISO registrars are certified to register to QS-9000, and not all ISO 9000 auditors are certified to audit to QS-9000. A list of registrars certified for QS-9000 as of January 1996 is included in Table 2.1.

Table 2.1   List of QS-9000 Approved Registrars as of January 1996

ABS Quality Evaluations ABS Plaza 16855 Northchase Drive Houston, TX 77060-6008 713-873-9400 713-874-9564 (fax) **(RvA and RAB approved)**	American Quality Assurance 1200 Main Street Suite M107 Columbia, SC 29201 803-779-8150 803-779-8109 (fax) **(RAB approved)**
AGA Quality 1425 Grand Vista Avenue Los Angeles, CA 90023 213-261-8161 213-261-3369 (fax) **(RAB approved)**	AT&T Quality Registrars 650 Liberty Avenue Union, NJ 07083 800-550-9001 908-851-3360 (fax) **(RAB approved)**

Table 2.1   List of QS-9000 Approved Registrars as of January 1996 (continued)

BSi Quality Assurance
Tysons Corner
8000 Towers Crescent Drive, Suite 1350
Vienna, VA 22182
703-760-7828
703-761-2770 (fax)
(RvA and UKAS approved)

BVQI
North American Central Offices
509 North Main Street
Jamestown, NY 14701
716-484-9002
716-484-9003 (fax)
(RAB approved)

BVQI (Netherlands)
North American Central Offices
509 North Main Street
Jamestown, NY 14701
716-484-9002
716-484-9003 (fax)
(RvA approved)

Det Norsk Veritas Certification
16340 Park Ten Place, Suite 100
Houston, TX 77084
713-579-9003
713-579-1360 (fax)
(RAB approved)

DNVI (Netherlands)
Det Norsk Veritas Certification
16340 Park Ten Place, Suite 100
Houston, TX 77084
713-579-9003
713-579-1360 (fax)
(RvA approved)

Entela QSRD
3033 Madison SE
Grand Rapids, MI 49548
616-247-0515
616-247-7527 (fax)
(RvA and RAB approved)

Intertek Services Corporation
9900 Main Street Suite 500
Fairfax, VA 22031
703-ISO-9000 ext. 3011
703-273-2895 (fax)
(RvA and RAB approved)

KPMG Quality Registrar
150 John F. Kennedy Parkway
Short Hills, NJ 07078-2778
800-716-5595
201-912-6050 (fax)
(RvA and RAB approved)

Lloyd's Register Quality Assurance
Norfolk House
Wellesley Road
Croydon, CR9 2DT
United Kingdom
01-81-688-682
01-81-681-8146 (fax)
(RvA approved)

Lloyd's Registrar Quality Assurance
33-41 Newark Street
Hoboken, NJ 07030
201-963-1111
201-963-3289 (fax)
(RAB approved)

NQA (Wales and Southwest England)
The QED Centre
Treforest Industrial Estate
Pontypridd, CF37 5YR
United Kingdom
01-44-384-4321
01-44-384-4345 (fax)
(UKAS approved)

NSF International
P.O. Box 130140
Ann Arbor, MI 48113-0140
313-769-6728
313-769-0109 (fax)
(RvA approved)

Enter QS-9000 37

Table 2.1 List of QS-9000 Approved Registrars as of January 1996 (continued)

OMNEX
880 South Grove
Ypsilanti, MI 48198
313-480-9940
313-480-9941 (fax)
(RAB approved)

QMI
Mississauga Executive Centre
Suite 800
2 Robert Speck Parkway
Mississauga, Ontario L4Z 1H8
Canada
905-272-3920
905-272-8503 (fax)
(RvA approved)

Quality Systems Registrars, Inc.
1373 Park Center Road Suite 217
Herndon, VA 22071-3279
703-478-0241
703-478-0645 (fax)
(RvA and RAB approved)

SGS International Certification Services
Canada Inc.
90 Gough Rd. Unit 4
Markham, Ontario L3R 5V5
Canada
905-479-1160
905-479-9452 (fax)
(RAB approved)

Smithers Quality Assessment
25 West Market Street
Akron, OH 44303-2099
216-762-4231
216-762-7447 (fax)
(UKAS approved)

Steel Related Industries Quality System
Registrar
2000 Corporate Drive Suite 450
Wexford, PA 15090
412-935-2844
412-935-6825 (fax)
(RvA and RAB approved)

TUV Essen
1032 Elwell Court Suite 222
Palo Alto, CA 94303
415-961-052
415-961-9119 (fax)
(RAB approved)

TUV Rheinland of N America
12 Commerce Road
Newton, CT 06470
203-426-0888
203-270-8883 (fax)
(RvA and RAB approved)

Certain accreditation bodies are recognized by Ford, General Motors, and Chrysler bodies. These national bodies approve registrars to conduct QS-9000 registrations. As of early 1996 the list included:

CL, Serrano, 240-7th Flr
Madrid, 28012 Spain
34-1457-3289
34-1458-6280 (fax)
(ENAC—Entidad Nacional de Acreditacion)

FINAS
P.O. Box 239
00181 Helsinki Finland
358-061-671
358-0616-7467 (fax)
(FINAS—Finland)

Table 2.1 List of QS-9000 Approved Registrars as of January 1996 (continued)

Japan Accreditation Board
Alaska Royal Bldg Anx
6-18 Alaska 7 Chrome, Minato-ku
Tokyo 107 Japan
81-3556-10375
81-3556-10376 (fax)
(JAB—Japan)

Justevesenet-Norwegian Metrology &
Accreditation Service
P.O. Box 6832 St. Olavs Plass
N-1030 Oslo Norway
47-22-200226
47-22-207772 (fax)
(NMAS—Norway)

Raad voor Accreditatie
Radboudwwartier 223
Postbus 2768
3500 GT Ufrecht Netherlands
31-30-239-45-00
31-30-239-45-39 (fax)
(RvA—Dutch Certification Council)

Registrar Accred Board
P.O. Box 3005
Milwaukee, WI 53201
800-248-1946 or
414-272-8575
414-765-8661 (fax)
(Registrar Accreditation Board—RAB)

SAS
CH-3084 Wabern
Lindenweg 50 Switzerland
41-31-963-3111
41-31-963-3210 (fax)
(SAS—Swiss Accreditation Service)

SINCERT
Via Battistotti Sassi 11
20133 Milano Italy
39-271-9202
39-271-9055 (fax)
(SINCERT—Italy)

Standard Council of Canada
45 O'Connor Street, Suite 1200
Ottawa, Ontario K1P 6N7 Canada
613-238-3222
613-995-4564 (fax)
(Standard Council of Canada—SCC)

SWEDAC
P.O. Box 878
SE-501 15
Boras, Sweden
46-33-177-745
46-33-101-392 (fax)
(SWEDAC—Sweden)

Tragergemeinschaft fur Akkrediterung
GMBH
Buro: Stresemannallee 13
60596 Frankfurt am Main Germany
49-69-630-2380
49-69-630-2365 (fax)
(TGA—Germany)

UKAS
Audley House
13 Palace Street
London SW1E 58HS
United Kingdom
44-171-233-7111
44-171-233-5115 (fax)
(UKAS)

Each of these accreditation bodies publishes lists of approved registrars for ISO 9000 and QS-9000.

In addition, there are also the requirements of the customer-specific section. Companies seeking registration will have to assure customer approval of control plans for General Motors, meeting heat-treating requirements for Ford, and the appropriate use of parts identified with symbols for Chrysler.

Developing a Checklist for the QS-9000 Audit

As noted above, developing a checklist for QS-9000 requires that a company reference three documents: the QS-9000 document itself, the sanctioned interpretations, and the QSA. In reading the QS-9000 requirements, remember that *shall, will,* and *must* indicate a mandatory requirement, whereas *should* indicates a preferred approach. Items labeled as "notes" are not requirements in either QS or ISO 9000. It is highly recommended that the process champion (whether ISO or QS) attend a sanctioned lead auditor course early in the preparation process. If this individual does not have auditing experience, it will help him or her "think like an auditor." If the individual has an auditing background, it will increase his or her understanding of the requirements and the "intent" of the standard.

As an example, a company preparing a checklist of Sections 4.1.2.1 and 4.1.3 (see Table 2.2 for the actual language of this standard) would first create its own checklist and then compare it to the QSA to assure that all relevant questions were identified.

This process forces the creator of the checklist to "think like an auditor" and answer two questions: "Do I have this requirement in place?" and "How can I prove that I have effectively implemented this element?" Some of the items on the audit checklist might include:

> Does the company have a quality policy? Is it known, understood, and implemented at all levels? How can this be verified?
>
> How is authority delegated to manage the quality system?
>
> Is the quality system reviewed? If yes, how often is it reviewed? What documentation do I have to demonstrate that these reviews are held? Are they dated and signed? Do they include all of the requirements? (Verify through checking meeting minutes.)

Table 2.2 Clauses from Management Responsibility Element 4.1 of QS-9000

Quality Policy—4.1.1	The supplier's management with executive responsibility shall define and document its policy for quality, including objectives for quality and its commitment to quality. The quality policy shall be relevant to the supplier's organizational goals and the expectations and needs of its customers. The supplier shall ensure that this policy is understood, implemented and maintained at all levels of the organization.
Organization—4.1.2	*Responsibility and Authority—4.1.2.1* The responsibility and authority and the interrelation of personnel who manage, perform and verify work affecting quality shall be defined and documented, particularly for personnel who need the organizational freedom and authority to: a) initiate action to prevent the occurrence of any nonconformities relating to product, process and quality system; b) identify and record any problems relating to the product, process and quality system; c) initiate, recommend or provide solutions through designated channels; d) verify the implementation of solutions; e) control further processing, delivery or installation of nonconforming product until the deficiency or unsatisfactory condition has been corrected.
Management Review—4.1.3	The supplier's management with executive responsibility shall review the quality system at defined intervals sufficient to ensure its continuing suitability and effectiveness in satisfying the requirements of this International Standard and the supplier's stated quality policy and objectives (see 4.1.1). Records of such reviews shall be maintained (see 4.16).

Preparing for the QS-9000 Audit

Preparing for a QS-9000 audit is no different than preparing for an ISO 9000 audit. In summary, the basic steps are to identify a cross-functional team, read through the standard clause by clause (including the sector- and customer-specific requirements), conduct a gap analysis (what a company currently has versus what is needed), develop a plan to close that gap, select an auditor, write policies and procedures, train everyone on the policies and procedures relevant to their job, conduct internal audits, correct the nonconformances noted, prepare for the pre-audit, and hold the audit. These steps are covered in depth in other sections of this book. The primary difference between the ISO audit and the QS-9000 audit is, obviously, that QS-9000 is far more comprehensive; thus, the documentation for compliance must be more extensive. Another difference, as previously noted, is that not all ISO 9000 registrars are approved as QS-9000 registrars. Check the list of registrars approved as of January 1996 to register firms to QS-9000 (Table 2.1) along with the certifying body (RvA, UKAS, RAB) before selecting your QS-9000 registrar.

The advantage of the QS-9000 process is the QSA. Using the QSA questions as a guide, a company can assure that, at least in terms of Section 1 and Parts of Section 2 of QS-9000, it is fully prepared for the audit. Essentially, the QSA provides a good part of the registrar's checklist. In preparing for the audit, the same rigor found in the QSA needs to be internally applied to Sections 2 and 3.

Recap

ISO 9000 is a subset of QS-9000. QS-9000 is more comprehensive than ISO 9000 in that it expands on the basic 20 ISO 9000 requirements and includes elements of continuous improvement and requirements for manufacturing capabilities. Whereas ISO 9000 has only one "section," QS-9000 has four: the ISO-based requirements, sector-specific requirements, customer-specific requirements, and the appendices. Not all ISO registrars are approved as QS-9000 registrars. Two advantages of seeking QS-9000 registration are the availability of "sanctioned interpretation" and the Quality System Assessment (i.e., generic QS-9000 checklist).

Chapter 3

Preparing for the ISO/QS-9000 Audit: Planning the Implementation

Learning Objectives

By the end of this chapter, you should be able to:

- Give two reasons why senior leadership must be deeply involved in the ISO/QS-9000 process
- List four topics that should be included in an executive briefing on ISO/QS-9000
- List the people (by function) who should be on the ISO steering committee
- Cite two advantages of benchmarking as related to ISO/QS-9000 registration

Introduction

To become registered to ISO/QS-9000, a company must start with two things: time and a plan. Wishes to the contrary, a company cannot achieve ISO or QS-9000 registration overnight. It takes time (depending on the size and procedural control of a company, possibly a great deal of time) to standardize existing procedures and make them conform to the ISO requirements, establish new procedures if necessary, train employees, and compile the documented history of compliance necessary to pass an ISO audit. The average company takes 12 to 18 months to prepare for and pass an ISO audit. Smaller companies, or those with highly developed quality programs, may be able to do it in less time.

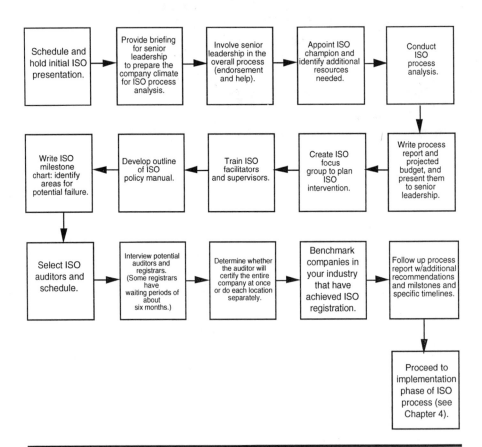

Figure 3.1 Preparing for the ISO Audit: Planning Implementation

Firms facing a great deal of outside pressure to become registered may be able to become registered faster by putting ISO implementation on the "fast track." Most registrars will not consider registering a company unless the company has at least six months of records indicating full implementation of its quality system. Companies with very complex processes or those with no outside pressure to become registered may take longer. Twelve to eighteen months is a reasonable projection to use in an initial presentation to senior leadership.

A detailed plan is also required. Just as no company would try to make a product without a detailed design and guidelines for every step in the process, no company should start the journey toward ISO registration without a road map. The more detailed the planning, the fewer changes to the system and revisions to procedures after implementation.

Figure 3.1 shows the first half of a typical process for obtaining ISO registration. While some of the steps or the order in which they appear may vary from company to company, most firms will follow this process in some form. This chapter covers the first half of the ISO implementation process: the planning phase. Chapter 4 details the second half of the process: putting the plan into action. (Chapters 3 and 4 focus on the efforts of a company rather than those of an outside consultant. Many companies find, however, that they need external help, at least in some areas. If a company decides to engage an outside consultant, it should be done as early in the implementation process as possible, and references should be checked.)

Initial Preparation

The ISO/QS registration process can begin at any number of places within a company. Sometimes it begins with a customer's remark to a sales representative or even to the CEO, indicating that the company needs to be preparing for ISO registration to maintain or improve the current level of the customer–supplier relationship. It can just as easily start when the manager of quality assurance hears from others that ISO likely will be a requirement for doing business with a number of customers in the coming years. For 15,000 suppliers of Ford, GM, and Chrysler, it began with a letter announcing a registration deadline for QS-9000. Regardless of where the push for ISO begins, one of the first steps in the process must be to provide an overall briefing for senior leadership— everyone on the executive committee.

Executive Endorsement

The question might be asked, "Why should we brief all of senior leadership? Do they really have to know what is going on?" The answer is a resounding *yes*. Unlike some other quality standards, ISO reaches beyond the shop floor and the inspection department. It reaches beyond calibration and shipping to purchasing and sales. It is not coincidence or mere courtesy that the first stop for many auditors during the actual ISO audit is to the office of the chief executive officer or president of the company. The operation of the quality system is ultimately the responsibility of the highest ranking officer in the firm. The CEO and other high-ranking officers need to understand this from the outset. Their involvement is critical throughout the process.

It is also important to involve senior leaders because, in many instances, some executive "encouragement" may be required with some managers or other employees. It is not unusual to find someone in management who simply refuses to cooperate with the changes needed to make a company meet the intent of the standard. Examples abound. In one case, an inside sales manager would not update his procedures or institute a customer complaint system until he was called into the office of the president and "encouraged" to cooperate in the ISO process. He was made to understand how important ISO registration was to the future of the company. In another case, a manager stated that he "had a department to run" and did not have time for this "quality stuff." This manager left the company because she simply could not handle the changes that needed to be made. In a third instance, a purchasing manager refused to share data about vendor performance with the quality assurance manager. Again, senior executive "persuasion" was required.

All of these examples point to the importance of keeping senior leadership not only informed of but committed to the ISO process. It is extremely difficult to achieve ISO registration without the active support and encouragement of the highest levels of the company. The attitudes and actions of each of the managers described above could have caused the company to receive a major nonconformance or even fail the audit.

Thus, one of the first steps in the process must be an executive briefing. This first briefing should be held with the CEO, president, CFO, and the highest ranking officers in all departments that will be affected directly by the ISO registration process. In most companies, this includes production, scheduling, purchasing, sales, customer service, quality, engineering, field service, training, and shipping. Topics covered in this presentation should include:

- An overview of ISO 9000
- An introduction to 9001, 9002, and 9003, highlighting significant differences among the three standards
- A brief description of each of the clauses in 9001 or 9002, depending on which standard the company will be seeking registration to
- The rationale for the company to seek registration
- Any cost figures already determined
- A review of the ISO registration process (as shown in Figure 3.1)
- An approximate time line for completion of registration
- Emphasis on the need for cooperation between and among departments in achieving registration
- Determination of the involvement of internal and external (a consultant, outside trainers, publications, software) support
- A question-and-answer period

It is important to remember that the goal of this presentation is not just to share information but to initiate the process. When the meeting is finished, everyone involved should be committed to pursuing ISO registration.

Think About It...

In your company, who should attend an initial ISO briefing? Why?

Appoint an ISO/QS-9000 Champion

Every company needs an ISO or QS-9000 "champion," someone who will assume responsibility for achieving registration and who will carry out or supervise the following activities:

- Coordinate with the steering committee
- Update senior leadership
- Help select the registrar
- Assist in writing the quality policy manual, standard operating procedures (SOPs), and job work instructions (JWIs)

- Work with the training department to translate the SOPs and JWIs into reality
- Manage the internal audit process
- Keep the process on track
- Coordinate all ISO-related activities
- Help maintain the documentation

Frequently the person selected for this job is the quality assurance manager, but it can be someone else. At a minimum, this person should have a direct reporting relationship to someone in executive management and should certainly be a participating member of the quality steering committee. The key is that the person meet the general requirements of the position. The person who is selected to head up the effort needs not only technical skills but also leadership and communication skills. It takes a lot of cooperation from others in the company to make the process work. A person who can only tell others to perform a task rather than ask and encourage them to do it, who gets so lost in the details of the operations that he misses the big picture, or who gets so taken with the vision that she cannot handle the details will have difficulty with the assignment.

The person selected for this task should be chosen carefully. The job should not be given to someone who simply has put in years of service and now has little to do. The person must have the clout and confidence to walk into the president/plant manager/general manager's office and share the results of the internal audit (even when these results are negative) and should also be able to communicate well with those who work on the shop floor. A recommended skill set for the ISO/QS champion is included in Table 3.1. Whoever is chosen, the selection should be made early in the process. ISO registration is a complicated and time-consuming process; the sooner the ISO champion is on board, the sooner the process can be started. The ISO champion is not necessarily the management representative, especially in large companies, but should report directly to the management representative.

Conduct an ISO/QS-9000 Process Analysis

A process analysis or "gap" (where the company is versus where it wants to be) analysis is a key element in the efficient planning of the ISO registration effort. An ISO process analysis essentially includes two facets: deciding which departments or functions are going to be included in the

Table 3.1 Qualifications of an ISO/QS-9000 Champion

While there are no hard and fast rules regarding the qualifications of the person who will lead the ISO process, a company should ask the following questions about a candidate for that position. Is the candidate:

1. Familiar with company systems and procedures?
2. Familiar with company organization?
3. Detail-oriented? Able to maintain files or supervise the maintenance of files?
4. Familiar with divisions/departments other than the one in which he or she currently works?
5. Able to work closely with senior leadership?
6. Able to relate to employees closest to the job?
7. Deadline oriented?
8. Well organized and tenacious?
9. A good communicator (both oral and written)?
10. Familiar with the auditing process?
11. Able to commit the time needed to complete the job?
12. A member of the company's management team or a direct report of the management team?

---

quality system (most companies will exclude the legal department, for example, and there are no specific requirements for the involvement of MIS or accounting except as they affect external customers) and determining the status of SOPs and JWIs that pertain to meeting the requirements of the various clauses.

Which departments or functions to include is a particularly important question if a company consists of more than one location (for example, corporate headquarters with satellite plants or smaller branches). If a company has multiple branches, it must decide how it wants to be registered. Does it want to register the company as a whole, or does it want to register the branches separately? (Multisite registration options are discussed later in this chapter.)

A company also must determine the status of current documented SOPs and JWIs. Many companies have SOPs for the production, shipping, handling, and inspection areas, but none for purchasing, customer service, inside sales, or other areas where SOPs are required by ISO. Unfortunately, many of the companies that have these procedures may find that they are either woefully out of date or just ignored by most of the people who are supposed to be using them. Some auditors will come back on the second and third shifts to assure that each person who performs a function follows the same SOPs and JWIs as his or her counterparts on other shifts. For example, an auditor might want to check that each draw bench operator sets up the dies and mandrels the same way or that each gauger uses the same JWI to check for wall thickness, inside diameter, or outside diameter.

Think About It...

What areas in your company have—and use—SOPs and JWIs?
In which areas do SOPs and JWIs need to be established?

Present Process Report to Senior Leadership

The results of the process analysis should be presented to the same group that approved the ISO/QS initiative. These leaders need to understand the extent of the effort required to achieve registration and the resources needed to achieve success. It is not unusual for senior management to be surprised at the status of SOPs within the company. They often assume that these procedures are not only current but also widely followed in daily operations. Regrettably, this is seldom the case.

Another reason to present this report to senior leadership is to convince those who manage functions such as purchasing and sales that they, too, must have SOPs and JWIs and that their people must follow them. For many purchasing departments, ISO is a whole new paradigm because it requires that purchasing decisions be based on criteria other than lowest price and that all suppliers need to meet predetermined quality requirements. Sales departments, especially those operating under the credo "whatever it takes to make the sale," also face a paradigm shift under ISO. For example, ISO 9001 Clause 4.3 requires that a company be certain it can meet all conditions of each contract—including delivery date—and be prepared to document that those requirements can, indeed, be met before a contract is accepted.

Create the ISO/QS-9000 Steering Committee for Initial Implementation

As stated above, the ISO/QS champion (whatever his or her actual title is) will lead the company's ISO efforts. However, that person will need some help. Within each company there are key individuals who can make a significant difference in the success of an ISO project if they understand the purpose and the process of ISO registration. These people should be organized into a group to help direct ISO activities. Whether this group of key individuals is called the ISO/QS steering committee, the ISO focus group, the ISO planning team, or any similar name, its job is to plan the ISO process and then to make certain that it happens.

Typically, this team consists of five to nine people, depending on the size of the company. In addition to the ISO champion, members include key personnel who will be essential to the success of the overall ISO registration effort. For example, MIS is typically represented on this committee. Even though MIS as a separate department may not be included in the ISO quality system, many quality processes within today's corporations are driven by the computer system. Many companies may have to do significant reprogramming to accommodate the ISO requirements, especially in such areas as quotations, sales, and purchasing.

It is also helpful to have someone from the training area on this team. Training has three roles in the ISO process. First, the training department will need to provide the on-the-job training needed to assure that everyone is trained in the newly written or newly updated SOPs and JWIs. Second, generalized training in the what, why, and how of ISO 9000 must be provided to all employees. (The amount of time allotted for this training varies from company to company; however, such a session would generally take about two to four hours.) Third, all employees need training in how to prepare for and participate in the audit process. They need to know, for example, that all questions asked by the auditor should be answered directly, honestly, and without expansion. The training department can prepare employees for this by conducting structured skill practices in which someone takes the role of auditor and asks questions based on current procedures and work instructions. (This training can be combined with the general ISO 9000 training listed above.)

In addition to representatives from MIS and training, the production, engineering, and service departments must be deeply involved. Because much of the ISO standards involve control of the company's key processes in one way or another, people from these critical areas need to be involved early on. Support services should also be included. ISO requires considerable documentation and record keeping. A company seeking registration needs to have a key person who will set up and/or maintain a records system that makes the audit process "auditor friendly."

All training must be documented, usually with a sign-in sheet, as evidence that the training actually occurred.

Train ISO/QS Facilitators

Every company with more than 60 employees will need a core of ISO leaders who will work directly with the ISO steering committee to spread ISO throughout the operation. These facilitators should be people from each area of the company who understand job functions and how to write SOPs and JWIs, who can train other employees in using new SOPs and JWI, and who can share the "message" of ISO with others. The ISO facilitators usually include department heads, but other key people, such as lead operators, should also be included. These people must be identified early in the ISO process.

Both steering committee members and facilitators need to be trained in the what, why, and how of ISO 9000 to be able to generate ideas as to how they can help the company implement the program. Topics include many of those listed in the executive briefing described above, as well as:

- Review of the key concepts of ISO 9004
- Information on how to write SOPs and JWIs
- Fundamentals of auditing
- Potential roadblocks to registration
- Three tiers of documentation (Policies, Procedures, and Work Instructions)
- Role of the facilitator in the registration process

This information may be presented in various ways. Some companies do it in a two-day workshop, for example, while others use a series of four-hour presentations. However the training is done, it is usually beneficial to include people who will not be part of the facilitator team but who may nevertheless be key in achieving registration.

Develop an Outline of the ISO/QS-9000 Quality Policy Manual

There is some confusion over what the term "quality policy manual" means. Some people use the term to describe the book that contains the company's quality policies. Others use "quality policy manual" or "quality manual" to describe the entire system of documentation needed to meet the intent of the standard. In this chapter, "quality policy manual" will be used to describe the book containing the company's quality policies. Writing the quality policy manual is not all that difficult or time consuming, once the concept of a manual is understood. The quality manual is essentially a response to the "shalls" of ISO. That is, ISO says, "you shall..." and the policy manuals says "we do..."

Because it is the first layer of documentation, the quality policy manual needs to be rather broad in its approach. Its purpose is to show, clause by clause, how the quality system of the company applying for registration will meet the intent of the standard. An example of a policy statement from an approved manual is shown in Figure 3.2. Obviously, a QS-9000 quality manual, because it must show commitment to a far broader range of requirements than ISO 9000, will be far more comprehensive.

For purposes of creating the outline for the quality policy manual, the best course is for members of the management team to read each clause, talk to the managers of the departments or areas where the content of that clause is appropriate, and ask them how, specifically, the intent of the standard is met within their areas. This information is then used for the initial outline. (The steps involved in assembling the manual and the other documentation needed are discussed in Chapter 4.) Management must be aware of the requirements of both QS and ISO prior to beginning to develop the quality manual. ISO offers guidelines for developing quality manuals in ISO 10013.

Create a Step-by-Step Plan

Creating a step-by-step plan for implementing ISO/QS-9000 and achieving registration is one of the most essential steps in assuring the efficient and timely achievement of the goal. While this process may seem intimidating at first glance, its importance cannot be overemphasized. The team may require as many as 30 hours to plan the process, but once the plan is in place, the ISO registration effort becomes a sequenced series of steps rather than a haphazard and random process of trying to get everything done at the same time.

Whichever planning tool is chosen by your team, it should address the following topics:

- What is the overall purpose of the process? What, other than attaining ISO/QS registration, is to be achieved by the registration

Port-O-Tech	Quality Policy 12	Section 12.0	Prepared by: CFS Date: 12-13-92	
	Subject: Control of Nonconforming Product	Effective Date Jan. 1, 1993	Rev. 0	Page 1 of 1

ORIGINATOR: Chief Executive Officer
RECIPIENTS: All Port-O-Tech Employees
SUBJECT: Control of Nonconforming Product
REFERENCES:
Procedure 0505 Equipment Problem Procedure
Procedure 0901 Purchasing: Criteria for Employing Horsepower
Procedure 0903 Incident Report Procedure
Procedure 1204 Investigative Procedure for Operations Incidents

12.1 General
Port-O-Tech has established procedures to identify nonconformities and ensure that appropriate action is taken. Nonconformities in the delivery of service are identified and reported through the daily incident reporting system. A nonconformity is defined as the failure of the system, activity, service process, or piece of equipment to comply with the specified requirements. The disposition of a nonconformity is the short-term action taken to deal with the nonconformity in order to continue service.

12.2 Review and Disposition of Nonconformities
Port-O-Tech maintains procedures for the review and disposition of nonconformities. Specific details as to the nature of the nonconformity are recorded to denote the actual conditions of the nonconformity. Procedures used during the review and disposition process include:
- Identification of the nonconformity
- Authority for the review of conditions surrounding the nonconformity
- Decision on disposition of the nonconformity

12.3 Responsibility
The manager of the area or department affected by the nonconformity, or his designated representative, is responsible for the disposition of the nonconformity.

J.C. Waxwell
Chief Executive Officer

Figure 3.2   ISO 9001 Requirements

effort (e.g., competitive advantage, improved process control, improved vendor quality)?
- What are the predictable outcomes or results of the process (e.g., standardization of production and customer service processes, reduction in number of vendors, lower cost of operation, reduced rework, ISO 9002 registration)?
- What should be measured (e.g., current levels of scrap and rework, vendor performance, rebills, time to process sales orders, cost of quality [see QS-9000])?
- Who are the internal and external customers and suppliers of this process (e.g., teams working on process improvement, the ISO registrar to be used, any external consultants to be used)?
- Where is the potential for failure of the process most likely and/or most serious (e.g., SOPs not followed, inadequate training on new procedures, procedures written without input from those closest to the process)?
- What are the most serious obstacles to success?
- Action steps: What needs to be done? By whom? When? How? Where? Why?
- What is needed for initial setup (materials, forms, planning, benchmarking, etc.)?
- What does an initial flow of the process look like?
- What is the time line for implementation? (Figure 3.3 shows a typical time line expressed in a milestone chart.)
- What are the anticipated tangible and intangible products (e.g., the quality policy manual, a companywide set of SOPs and JWIs, improved customer satisfaction, ISO registration certificate)?
- Which job functions or areas will be key to the process? (The manager of quality assurance or the ISO champion will be one of these key roles.)
- What types of training will be necessary to achieve the objective? (As noted above, training is a key element in the overall ISO process. Table 3.2 shows some of the training that may be required.)
- How will the team ensure that the plan is being followed? (Will there be an audit? Will someone assume the responsibility? How often will the team meet to track progress?)

Activity	Oct	Nov	Dec	Jan	Feb	Mar	Apr	May	Jun	Jul	Aug	Sep	Oct	Nov	Dec	Jan	Feb	Mar	Apr
Management empowers ISO.	■	■																	
Select ISO champion.		■	■																
Select auditing firm.			■	■	■														
Write quality strategic initiative for ISO.				■	■														
Collect existing documentation and procedures					■	■													
Determine what company needs to do for ISO registration.					■	■													
Develop process for writing SOPs and JWIs.						■	■												
Make employees aware of ISO thrust.								■	■	■	■	■	■	■	■	■	■	■	
Write quality policy manual							■	■											
Write SOPs.								■	■	■	■	■	■						
Set up document control procedures.									■	■									
Collect data.										■	■	■	■	■	■	■	■	■	
Write JWIs.											■	■	■						
Write systems manual.													■	■					
Conduct ISO training for all employees.														■	■	■	■	■	
Conduct internal audits and fix nonconformances.													■	■					
Conduct pre-audit and fix nonconformances.																		■	
Conduct final audit.																			■

Figure 3.3 Sample Time Line for ISO Implementation (Obviously, additional steps would be required for QS-9000 due to its more comprehensive nature.)

Table 3.2 Suggested Training for ISO/QS Implementation

I. Training the trainer for SOPs and JWIs
Instructional Objectives
To train department heads and branch managers in the use of SOPs and JWIs. The department heads and branch managers will then train their employees (cascade training).

Skills Needed
Those necessary to perform the job functions

Concepts to Be Taught
1. Importance of following the SOPs and JWIs
2. Consequences to the company if people do not comply with SOPs and JWIs
3. How the SOPs and JWIs relate to the quality policies
4. How a policy, an SOP, and a JWI fit together so the employee can do his or her job
5. The "why" of our pursuit of QS-9000 registration—it is not an option

II. Train the auditors for Quality System Audit
Instructional Objectives
Learn how to audit a company's quality system.

Skills Needed
1. Familiarity with audit process
2. Interview skills
3. Knowledge of the company's quality system

Concepts to Be Taught
1. Intent of ISO/QS-9000 standards
2. How to audit compliance with the standards

III. Training on SOPs and JWIs for department heads and branch managers
Instructional Objectives
To provide an understanding of how a company's policies, procedures, and work instructions fit together and what purposes they serve.

Skills Needed
No additional skills are needed

Concepts to Be Taught
Same as the instructional objectives

IV. Training on Document and Data Control
Instructional Objectives
To provide an understanding of why and how documents are controlled.

Skills Needed
No additional skills are needed

Table 3.2   Suggested Training for ISO/QS Implementation (continued)

Concepts to Be Taught
1. ISO requirements for document and data control
2. How the company's document and data control system complies with the standards
3. Procedures to be followed when documents and data need to be changed

V. Employee Training on New Procedures
Instructional Objectives
To train employees on how to use the company's SOPs and JWIs.

Skills Needed
Those necessary to do the job

Concepts to Be Taught
The step-by-step process to do the job

It is particularly important at this time to identify the potential barriers to a successful effort. For example, ISO 9001 Clause 4.11 requires that all calibrated equipment used in critical operations be calibrated on a regular schedule. The equipment should be marked or tagged in a manner that allows the auditor to quickly verify that, indeed, this piece of equipment has been calibrated according to a set schedule. A problem sometimes occurs when equipment is owned by the operator or mechanic rather than by the company, which frequently happens in companies that do field repairs. The company will religiously maintain its calibration schedule for in-house equipment, but equipment owned by repair personnel is often overlooked. The company must take steps to ensure that *all* equipment used in critical operations is tagged or marked with a number and regularly calibrated to a known standard. Problems of this nature can occur in almost every area of every company. They must be anticipated if the registration effort is to proceed smoothly.

Deciding Upon Registration

The problem of selecting a registrar is extensive. Questions such as cost, scope, where the registrar's mark is accepted, and other considerations must be examined. The topic is so far-ranging that Chapter 5 is devoted to interviewing and selecting the registrar.

Multisite Registration

Early in the process, a multisite or multibranch company must decide whether it will be registered as a single entity or whether each site (or each region or each functional group) will be registered separately. There are no easy answers to this question. Each company must decide the question for itself, based on its own unique circumstances.

Normally, if there is a corporate office/plant with one or two nearby satellite offices/ plants that essentially do the same thing as the corporate office/plant, the entire unit can receive registration as one unit, if that best suits the company's needs and the desires of its customers. If a company's branches are small (less than 10 percent of the number of employees at the main office) and have no customers asking for ISO, it may not make sense to register them at all. If the branches are large and need to be registered but do things differently than the main or corporate office, the company has several options: to register as one company, to register headquarters only, or to register headquarters and register most or all of the branches later (a "scope extension"). If a company registers its branches separately, it does not have to register them all to the same standard. If, for example, all design work is done at headquarters and other sites are production facilities, then it would make sense for the company to have the sites registered separately to ISO 9002, while headquarters is registered to 9001.

Take, for example, the chemical giant DuPont. Each of its plants, most with a unique function, is registered separately. The large branches with design functions are registered to ISO 9001, while the process plants are registered to ISO 9002. On the other hand, Mayer Electric Supply, an electric parts distributor with offices throughout Alabama, Georgia, Tennessee, and Florida, all of which rely on headquarters for most support activities, became registered as a single entity first with corporate, then with the branches on a "scope extension."

The question can be especially difficult for the second wave of ISO registration applicants, the suppliers to the major manufacturing firms that received registration during 1993, 1994, and 1995. These suppliers are frequently smaller manufacturing operations, distributors/wholesalers, and packing/shipping operations.

QS-9000 as a Separate Registration

Because the first half of QS-9000 is ISO 9000, achieving QS-9000 registration is evidence that a company has met the ISO 9000 requirements.

Specifically, QS-9000 registration assures nonautomotive companies that the QS-9000-registered supplier has met the requirements of ISO 9001 or 9002. Of course, the opposite is not true. ISO registration is not evidence of having met the QS-9000 requirements.

To Combine or Not to Combine

Many industrial distributors are not only multisite operations; their sites may also vary widely in the number of employees and the actual services provided. Sometimes it is difficult to decide whether to combine these operations or have them registered separately. While each company will have its own particulars, a sample case may provide some guidance.

A distributor of pipe valves and fittings with its main offices in Houston has branch operations in Texas City, Tyler, Freeport, and Beaumont, Texas, as well as Lake Charles and Baton Rouge, Louisiana. While the main office (or "mother branch") in Houston has over 200 employees, the outlying branches range in size from 6 to 57 employees. The Houston office was receiving some pressure from customers in the chemical and process industries to achieve ISO registration, as were the operations in Texas City, Freeport, and Baton Rouge.

After consulting with the registrar it had selected, the company decided to use the main branch as a pilot operation and achieve registration there first. Therefore, the company designed its quality policy manual to fit the entire operation but wrote the procedures and work instructions to fit operations only at the main location. Once registration was achieved at the main branch, procedures and work instructions were adapted where necessary for the other branches (i.e., in the smaller branches there were no specific staging areas for orders to be shipped, as there was at the main branch), and the Texas City, Freeport, and Baton Rouge operations were registered. This company decided that, while all SOPs and JWIs would be adopted by all branches for internal quality purposes, it made no economic sense to register the branches that were smaller (six employees) and were receiving no customer pressure to achieve registration.

The decision on how to register a multisite operation is a difficult one and depends on a number of factors, including cost (registering even a small one-site operation may cost about $9,000; one registrar's proposal for registering a company with 20 outlying branch offices was in excess of $100,000). This decision should be made in conjunction with the registrar the company selects or as part of the process of selecting the registrar. That is, it is acceptable to explain the company's situation to the registrar and ask how registration should be approached—and how much it would cost the company if registration were achieved that way.

Think About It...
If your company has multiple sites, should it register each site separately or register the company as a whole?

Benchmark Companies That Have Achieved ISO or ISO QS-9000 Registration

Benchmarking is a practical activity in ISO implementation. Examining what another company did to standardize its procedures, create a documentation system, and perform other activities central to ISO registration will give you some ideas on how to implement ISO in your own company. Benchmarking saves a company from having to reinvent the wheel.

Skeptics have been heard to say, "My competitors aren't going to let me see what they did to become registered." While this may be true, it does not mean that benchmarking is useless. Because ISO 9000 is designed to apply to almost every industry—as are quality principles—a company can learn a lot from benchmarking ISO-registered companies in seemingly unrelated fields.

For example, while a company may not learn much from a firm in a different field in terms of those clauses that pertain directly to process control, much can be learned from benchmarking in terms of document control, purchasing, contract review, corrective action, training, and control of nonconforming product. It is also a good idea to review a quality policy manual from a company that has achieved ISO registration. While quality policy manuals differ from company to company, the good ones are based on principles that can be applied to any company.

A good example of this "generic benchmarking," although not done specifically for ISO 9000, occurred between IBM and L.L. Bean. Although the two companies would seem to have little in common on the surface, IBM identified L.L. Bean as a leader in order fulfillment and warehousing and benchmarked those operations in order to improve its own procedures in those areas.

It is important not to approach benchmarking as a trivial visit. Plan ahead. In the most successful benchmarking efforts, more time is spent on planning the visit than on the actual trip. Get input from all areas of your operation concerning what specific areas should be studied. Go prepared with a list of specific areas or functions to visit and a specific agenda. Do not be afraid to ask questions. Remember, procedures for corrective action and document control can often be adapted across industries. A company that makes steel can learn something from a company that services phones if the benchmarking visit is carefully thought out beforehand.

When the visit is completed, the benchmarking team should meet to discuss what was learned and how that information can be adapted to fit the company. The team should not be afraid to propose changes in the company's ISO plan or milestone calendar to accommodate the new information.

One last suggestion for benchmarking: Don't be afraid to ask the company being benchmarked for materials. Many companies are justifiably proud of what they have done to achieve ISO registration. They may give examples of policies, procedures, work instructions, and record-keeping forms to noncompetitors.

Think About It...

What are some companies in your area that would make good benchmarking partners?

Once benchmarking is completed, the ISO steering committee may need to revise its timetable, objectives, and/or methods. This revision, if needed, is the last step in the ISO planning process. It is now time to put the plan in action throughout the company. The action phase of ISO implementation and registration is discussed in Chapter 5.

Recap

ISO/QS-9000 registration takes both time and a detailed plan. A company must start by involving senior leadership, both because ISO 9000 requires the involvement of top management and because the ISO 9000 process is not likely to succeed if top management does not wholeheartedly endorse it. From this level, ISO concepts are expanded throughout the operation, to an ISO/QS-9000 champion and steering committee, to ISO facilitators in each department, and, finally, to each worker. Training is essential to a successful ISO effort. Top management, the ISO champion, and the ISO facilitators should receive intensive training in the what, how, and why of ISO 9000, and every employee should be exposed to the general concepts of ISO 9000. A multisite company must decide if it will be registered as a single entity or have each site registered separately. A company should benchmark ISO-registered companies to learn how they overcame problems in ISO implementation.

Chapter 4

Preparing for the ISO/QS-9000 Audit: Putting the Plan into Action

Learning Objectives

By the end of this chapter, you should be able to:

- List three functions that should be included in a company's quality system
- Name several types of documents that should be included in a company's quality records
- Cite three functions of document control
- List three guidelines for internal quality audits

Introduction

Chapter 3 discussed the early stages of ISO/QS-9000 implementation—involving senior leadership, selecting an ISO champion and a steering committee, training facilitators, deciding on multisite registration, and benchmarking. This chapter continues with the ISO implementation process. (Figure 4.1 shows the second half of the ISO implementation process.)

Creating the Quality Manual and Documentation System

As stated in Chapter 3, the quality manual and documentation system maintained to verify implementation of the system are the keys to ISO or QS-9000 registration. Thus, they require a great deal of planning. Questions that should be addressed include:

- What existing systems/departments should be included in the quality system?
- Which existing systems/departments should not be included?
- Which functions or procedures need to be altered to meet the intent of the standard?
- What new systems need to be created to meet the requirements of the standard?
- What will be included in the quality manual?
- What records must be maintained in order to meet the requirements of the standard?
- Who will write the quality manual?
- What document control procedures need to be implemented to meet the intent of the standard?

Defining the Quality System

Most companies initially define their quality systems in very narrow terms, limiting the system to production or sometimes just to inspection or quality control. ISO and QS-9000, on the other hand, have a very broad definition of a quality system: "The organizational structure, responsibilities, processes, procedures and resources for implementing quality management." Thus, companies must examine their operations to determine what areas previously left out of the quality system should be included for purposes of ISO.

Preparing for the ISO/QS-9000 Audit: Putting the Plan into Action

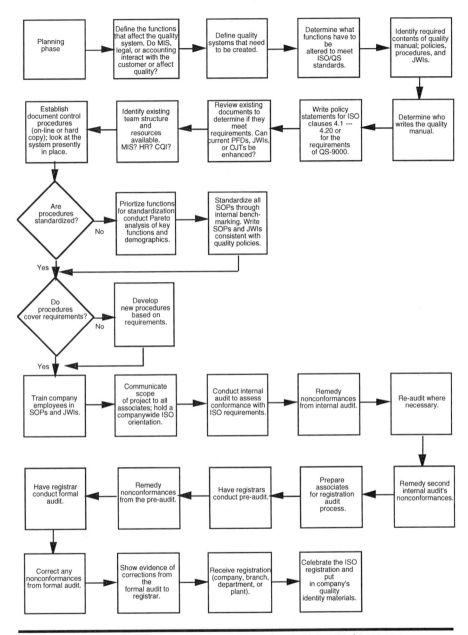

Figure 4.1   Preparing for the ISO Audit: Implementing ISO/QS-9000

Most companies seeking registration to ISO and/or QS-9000 must examine more than just those functions that are usually thought to affect quality. While some functions are specifically mentioned in the standards and have definite requirements placed upon them (for example, production, purchasing, shipping, R&D, and training), others are not mentioned and must be inferred. Inside sales is one example. Sales representatives who take orders over the phone can have a big effect on quality as it affects the customer, even if they never meet the customer face to face. The quality system required for QS-9000 is far wider in scope than that required by ISO 9000. Contents of the QS-9000 quality manual are discussed in greater depth later in this chapter.

Of course, some functions have no direct effect on quality as it applies to the customer. The most common of these functions involves the legal department. Another involves MIS. Although it is true that MIS will play a major role in ISO implementation (an increasing number of companies keep their quality manuals and records electronically rather than on paper), MIS procedures generally do not affect the customer directly. Many companies also choose not to include accounting in the quality system. Some accounting functions (most notably accounts payable) may have some effect on quality, but this effect may be accommodated by including these functions as part of another area.

What Functions Must Be Altered to Meet the Intent of the Standard?

In almost every company, some functions or processes must be altered in order to comply with the intent of either ISO 9000 or QS-9000. In some cases, only minor adjustments will be necessary. Other areas, however, may require some fundamental changes.

Purchasing

The purchasing department usually must change to comply with ISO standards. In many companies, purchasing is the last department to adopt quality principles; it continues to make decisions based on low price or long-term relationships. Top management unwittingly supports this practice by praising purchasing for making "great deals," by insisting on strict attention to the bottom line, or by setting up competing profit centers within the same company. Unfortunately, some of these "great deals" turn out to be not so great because the cut-rate material does not meet the

Preparing for the ISO/QS-9000 Audit: Putting the Plan into Action **69**

requirements of the company's manufacturing process and must be reworked before it can be used. The bottom line on these deals can often be higher (that is, cost the company more money) than if the company had paid a higher price for material that met its specifications.

ISO 9001 Clause 4.6 is very specific about purchasing requirements; it requires that companies establish and maintain a list of approved vendors. (Not surprisingly, QS-9000 takes this even further, specifying that relevant materials shall be purchased from subcontractors on the approved vendor list.) The vendors are to be selected on the basis of how their products meet the company's requirements. This can be determined by past records, receiving inspections, statistical input from the supplier, or second-party or third-party audits, as long as the means of determination is documented in the company's quality records. ISO 9004 suggests that a company limit the number of suppliers and establish long-term relationships with them.

Sales

Another area that may require considerable change to meet the intent of the standard is sales. Many companies operate, whether officially or unofficially, by the credo "whatever it takes to get the sale." Unfortunately, this attitude too often means that sales representatives will promise things that the company simply cannot deliver—a certain level of quality, a certain price, or, frequently, a certain delivery date. While this behavior is done not maliciously but rather out of enthusiasm or eagerness to get the sale, meet a quota, or achieve a forecast, it definitely impacts "quality as it affects the customer."

ISO 9001 and QS-9000 address this in Clause 4.3, Contract Review. This clause calls for each contract to be reviewed to determine that: (1) the requirements are adequately defined and documented, (2) any requirements differing from those in the initial contract/bid/quote (either written or verbal) are resolved, and (3) the supplier has the capability to meet contractual requirements. These requirements ensure that a supplier does not promise what it cannot deliver and, conversely, that a customer does not base its future delivery schedule on promises which the supplier simply cannot fulfill.

In one company, for example, the policy had been for sales representatives to promise a one- or two-day delivery even when they knew that two or three weeks might be the best the company could do. After the product was shipped, the sales department would adjust the file, changing the promise date to match the actual delivery date. A long history of this practice led customers to ask for unreasonable delivery dates in the hope of getting delivery in a reasonable amount of time. In implementing ISO, this company made a bold decision—it would quote only realistic delivery dates, would do no "file maintenance," and would publish accurate data regarding actual delivery. The company would work with customers and suppliers to improve on-time delivery. The plan worked. This example shows how ISO can be used as a vehicle for continuous quality improvement.

Top management must take the lead in "encouraging" both purchasing and sales to abide by the ISO requirements. In purchasing, this means reducing the emphasis on price and focusing instead on total cost. In sales, this may mean taking a temporary "hit" while the company reestablishes a sense of "delivery integrity" with its customers. However it is done, top management must take a leading role.

Think About It...

What functions in your company will need serious alteration to meet ISO standards? What about these functions needs to be changed?

Contents of the Quality Manual

As discussed earlier, there is some confusion as to what the term *quality manual* means. Some people use the term to describe the one book which contains the company's quality policies. Others use it to describe the entire system of documentation needed to meet the intent of the standard. For the purposes of this book, three terms will be used. *Quality policy manual* (or *policy manual*) will be used to describe the book (often a three-ring binder) containing the company's quality policies. *Documentation* will be used to describe the standard operating procedures, job work instructions, and quality records that support those policies. *Documentation system* will be used to describe both the quality policy manual and documentation. Another term frequently heard is Tier 1, Tier 2, and Tier 3. For our purposes, Tier 1 is the quality policy manual, Tier 2 is the procedures, and Tier 3 is the work instructions.

Quality Policy Manual

The quality policy manual is the backbone of a company's ISO/QS-9000 registration effort. Policies set out a company's commitment to quality and customer satisfaction and state how a company is going to go about realizing that commitment.

The first policy in the manual sets the stage for the others. Generally known as a *quality mission statement* (or "quality policy"), it outlines the company's overall commitment to quality and customer service. The quality mission statement is a key element in a living, dynamic quality system as required by ISO and QS-9000. It should be signed by the CEO to show management's commitment to the principles outlined therein, in compliance with Clause 4.1, Management Responsibility. It is a good idea for all senior leaders to sign the quality mission statement; doing so lends credence to the company's quality commitment. In some companies, the quality mission statement is signed by all employees as a sign of their commitment to quality. (This should be done only on a voluntary basis.) Incidentally, a frequent first question from an auditor to an employee is, "What is the company's quality statement and what does it mean to you?"

The policies in the quality policy manual delineate a company's commitment to quality in different aspects of its operation. Most companies have a quality policy for each aspect of their operation as defined by ISO 9000—one for Purchasing, one for Contract Review, one for Process Control, and so on. If you are writing policies from scratch, it is a good idea to number them according to the ISO standards. The policy on management responsibility, for example, would be designated Policy 4.1, because management responsibility is covered under Clause 4.1. The policy on the quality system would be Policy 4.2, and so on. Companies with existing policies (and an existing numbering system) should cross-reference those policies to the ISO 9000 requirements. (Cross-referencing is not specifically required by ISO 9000, but it makes the documents easier for the auditor to locate.) Figure 4.2 shows a sample of a quality policy.

A company planning to register its branches, sites, or plants separately may have a quality policy manual and documentation system for each site or may use the corporate manual with different procedures and work instructions. The branch policies may be virtually identical to headquarters' policies, although they may reflect differences in operations. The best example of this is a company where all design and contract review functions are conducted at headquarters, and the branches are merely manufacturing or processing facilities. Thus, headquarters would have

HM	Quality Policy 5	Rev.	Prepared by: CFS Date: 12-13-91		
	Subject: Identification & Traceability Control	Effective Date Jan. 1, 1992	Section	Page 1 of 1	

ORIGINATOR: Chief Executive Officer
RECIPIENTS: All HM Employees
SUBJECT: Control of Nonconforming Product

5.1 General

This section establishes the control and identification of material throughout the manufacturing process and during shipment. The individual items of production are permanently marked with a traceable number or machined to a unique part number with a traceable number that is readily associated with the process, inspection, and test reports. These numbers are referred to as the part number and the heat number.

5.2 Identification Requirements

Upon receipt of a customer order, an individual, unique sales order number will be assigned to it. In addition to the production order number, an individual part number and unique serial number is assigned. These numbers will be the identity for the customer's order throughout the manufacturing process. In-process identification may be stamped or painted on the parts. Final marking information such as part number, size, flange rating, pressure/vacuum setting, capacity, and serial number shall be stamped on a stainless steel nameplate and permanently affixed to the unit.

5.3 Identification Traceability

Identification of completed material is identified with the material certification, when required, by the part number and serial number. Where a certificate of conformance or certificate of tests is required, each are traceable to the part number and serial number.

5.4 Method of Marking

Material shall be marked by any method acceptable to the purchaser that will not result in any harmful contamination or sharp discontinuities and will identify the material in accordance with the material specification. Stamping, when used, will be done with blunt-nosed continuous-dot or blunt-nosed interrupted-dot die stamps.

5.5 Welding Material Identification

Welding materials received from the vendor shall be verified by the welding lead person to have been clearly identified on the container or package with:
- Heat or lot number
- Specification
- Classification number
- Control marking code
- Grade
- Supplier's name and trade designation

N. B. Scott
Chief Executive Officer

Figure 4.2 Sample of Quality Policy

Preparing for the ISO/QS-9000 Audit: Putting the Plan into Action 73

Quality Policy Manual	
13.0 CONTROL OF NONCONFORMING PRODUCT	
13.1	General
*	HM has documented procedures to identify nonconformities and to ensure that appropriate action is taken. Nonconformities in the delivery of service are identified and reported through the daily incident reporting system. A nonconformity is defined as a failure of the system, activity, service process, or piece of equipment to comply with specified requirements. The disposition of a nonconformity is the short-term action taken to deal with the nonconformity in order to continue service.
13.2	Review and Disposition of Nonconformities
•	HM maintains documented procedures for the identification, review, and disposition of nonconformities. Specific details as to the nature of the nonconformity are recorded to denote the actual conditions of the nonconformity. Procedures used during the review and disposition process include: • identification of the nonconformity • authority for the review of conditions surrounding the nonconformity • decision on disposition of the nonconformity
13.3	Responsibility
•	The manager of the area or department affected by the nonconformity, or his designated representative, is responsible for the disposition of the nonconformity.
•	Reference: Maintenance and Repair Procedure Manual Traffic Procedure Manual Vessel Operations Procedure Manual

Doc./Sec. No.: 0100-12	Issued: 03/01/95	Approved by: Sanders
Revision No.: 02	Page 1 of 1	Written by: Gonzales

Figure 4.2 Sample of Quality Policy (continued)

policies on design control and contract review, but the branches would not. (Each branch's quality policy manual would simply state, "4.4 Design Control: All Design Control functions are handled at the headquarters in East Springfield.")

The QS-9000 Policy Manual

As mentioned in Chapter 2, QS-9000 is broader in scope than ISO in that it includes the ISO 9001 requirements plus additions to these requirements, plus continuous improvement activities, plus manufacturing capabilities, plus customer-specific requirements. Obviously, this means that the typical QS-9000 Tier 1 policy manual is going to be more comprehensive than its ISO 9000 counterpart. Remember, the purpose of the Tier 1 manual is to answer each of the "thou shalt" requirements of the clauses within the standard with a response of "we do" (not "we will do").

For example, ISO 9002, Section 4.3.1 reads, "The supplier shall establish and maintain documented procedures for contract review and for the coordination of these activities." A company seeking registration assures its customers that it has such procedures in its policy manual with a statement such as: "Triliner Manufacturing has developed and maintains documented procedures for contract review and assures that activities surrounding contract review (including contract approval and contract amendment) are coordinated." This statement demonstrates that Triliner is committed to this process and that it has documented procedures which the auditor can examine in order to verify compliance.

Because QS-9000 has more than five times as many pages of requirements as ISO in its three sections, a supplier has a wider range of commitments to make. Do not overlook any requirement unless it is a "Does not Apply." Auditors look for compliance with all aspects of the system, not just selected clauses.

Standard Operating Procedures and Job Work Instructions

It may help to think of the documentation system as a pyramid, with each layer supported by the broader layers beneath it. Figure 4.3 shows an example of pyramid documentation. The quality policies, including the company's overall quality mission statement, are at the top. Supporting the policies is the second level, standard operating procedures (SOPs), which in turn are supported by the third tier, job work instructions

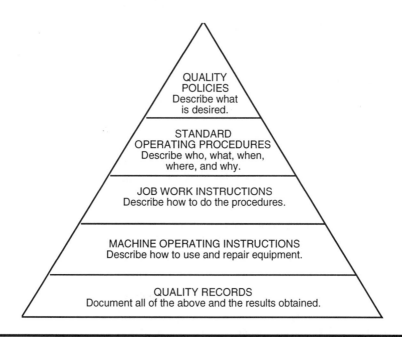

Figure 4.3 Pyramid Documentation Used in Establishing a Quality System

(JWIs). The bottom two tiers are machine operating instructions and quality records.

Some companies tend to blur the distinction between SOPs and JWIs and call everything a "procedure." In many companies, however, they are different. (The most notable exceptions are very small companies and those with a sophisticated work force, such as engineering firms.) The auditor will expect to see documentation that is sufficiently detailed to assure control of the process, whether it be in a very detailed procedure or a set of SOPs supported by JWIs.

The differences between an SOP and a JWI can best be explained with this example from an emergency vendor approval procedure which meets part of the requirement for Clause 4.6 of ISO 9001. In this case, the documentation pyramid begins with the company policy statement (4.6), which says, "International Warehouse and Lighting Supply Company has established and maintains standard operating procedures...for all activities involving the purchasing of supplies and equipment." The second layer of the pyramid is the SOP. This SOP begins with a salesperson needing an emergency vendor approval, usually in response to a specific customer request. The salesperson notifies purchasing, which finds the vendor for the item and seeks to verify product liability requirements. While waiting for the indemnification agreement from the emergency vendor, the salesperson contacts accounting, which faxes a copy of the company's credit information to the prospective vendor. Before the action covered by the SOP is completed, sales, purchasing, accounting, and credit have all been involved.

Now let's consider the JWI (the third layer of the pyramid) that accompanies and supports this SOP. Step 6.10 of the JWI explains how to order the material from the conditionally approved vendor. It is very specific:

6.10.1 Salesperson contacts vendor and places order. Salesperson will follow JWI 452, 371, or 504, depending on whether this is a back-order or a direct purchase.

6.10.2 Salesperson prepares a handwritten purchase order.

6.10.3 Salesperson completes "Emergency Supplier Request Form."

6.10.4 Record salesperson's name in Block A.

6.10.5 Record the customer's name in Block B.

6.10.6 Continues.

As this example shows, the JWI is far more detailed than the SOP. There is generally a JWI for each of the steps (or at least the more involved steps) in each SOP.

Each policy is supported by a number of procedures, which in turn are supported by a number of work instructions. It is essential that the numbering system devised for policies, SOPs, and JWIs reflect that relationship. The best way to do this is to use an "add-on" numbering system. For example, if inspection and testing is covered under Policy 4.10, then the procedure for receiving inspections (the first inspection done) would be designated 4.10.1. The work instruction for unloading the truck (the first step in the receiving inspection procedure) would be designated 4.10.1.1.

The fourth tier of the pyramid (where applicable) is composed of machine operating instructions. These are the reference manuals that come from the manufacturer, sometimes appended by the company's operators. They tell how to adjust the machine's settings and provide general operating information. This information is sometimes, but not necessarily, included in JWIs. Machine operating instructions should be kept near the machine to which they pertain so that operators will have access to them when needed.

Think About It...

Does your company currently have all the SOPs and JWIs required by ISO 9000 or QS-9000? How would you go about deciding what procedures or work instructions need to be added?

Quality Records

The bottom of the pyramid consists of quality records. This is a catchall category that includes all documents that provide evidence of how a company has implemented its quality policies. Some documentation categories are required specifically by ISO 9001. Others serve as proof that actions called for in a company's quality policies did, indeed, take place. Quality records typically include the following:

- Minutes of quality-related meetings
- Contracts (with sign-offs from review sessions; required by ISO 9001 Clause 4.3)
- Product designs (with sign-offs from review sessions) (required by ISO 9001 Clause 4.4)
- Records from suppliers (required by ISO 9001 Clause 4.6)
- Product identification records (required by ISO 9001 Clause 4.8)
- Test and inspection results (required by ISO 9001 Clause 4.10)
- Calibration records for inspection, measuring, and test equipment (required by ISO 9001 Clause 4.11)
- Results of internal quality audits (required by ISO 9001 Clause 4.17)
- Training records (required by ISO 9001 Clause 4.18)
- Statistical process control charts (ISO Clause 4.20)

ISO requires that quality records be "readily retrievable." Each company defines what that means. In a small company, "readily retrievable" may mean the person in charge of quality records can walk over to a filing cabinet and select the desired document. In very large corporations, "readily retrievable" may mean that the records can be located in a week or less. The key to registration is that a company be able to defend the practicality of its definition to the auditor and live up to that definition.

Think About It...

Name three types of documents that should be included in your company's quality records, according to ISO 9000. Does your company currently keep these records?

Who Will Write the Quality Manual?

Once the contents of the quality policy manual and other documentation have been determined, a company must decide who will compile the material. A company has several choices, but the best method for most firms is to have the ISO champion or the quality manager do the initial draft of information from workers from all areas of the operation. This recommendation is based on a simple fact: ISO requires that a company's quality documentation accurately reflect its quality system; that is, that it show how things are really done. If a company is starting from scratch, it makes sense to write the policy statements in a format consistent with ISO. If a company is integrating existing policies into the ISO framework, it should make certain that the policies are consistent with ISO. In either case, the company should involve in writing the policy statement the people who manage the processes covered by each clause of ISO. If you integrate ISO policies into an existing manual, remember to make it auditor friendly. Create a matrix to show where the statement of compliance can be found for each section of the requirements.

The ISO auditor will examine the company's documentation to see that it meets this criterion and will question workers to determine if they follow the written procedures and instructions. Procedures and work instructions written by an outside consultant, no matter how good a writer he or she may be, are not likely to be a true reflection of a company's processes. The same is true of having the ISO champion perform the task by himself or herself. One person is not likely to be familiar with all the operations in any company with more than a handful of workers. The result will be procedures and work instructions that do not accurately portray how tasks are performed. Therefore, the team approach is the best choice. Whereas department managers frequently sign off on or approve procedures and work instructions that affect their department, final approval of the Tier 1 manual should come from executive-level personnel.

Get Input from Those "Closest to the Job"

The ISO/QS-9000 champion should meet with managers and workers from each area of the company and get their input on how tasks are performed. The first step is to review existing procedures and work instructions to determine if they meet ISO requirements.

- Are they written or just "understood"?
- Are they standard throughout the company?
- Are they clear and concise?
- Do they support the intent of the standard?
- Are the practices therein compatible with the ISO requirements?

In most companies, existing procedures and work instructions will need some revamping to meet the intent of ISO. New procedures and instructions will undoubtedly need to be written. In both cases, the ISO champion—"designated writer"—should write the procedures and work instructions with input from those closest to the job and then submit them to the same workers for review and, if needed, revision. The ISO champion also may be able to draw upon any existing work teams, as well as MIS, human resources, and the quality department. This team approach ensures that the procedures and work instructions produced will be the ones that are followed throughout the plant.

Enhance Procedures with Process Flow Diagrams

It is a good idea to create a process flow diagram (PFD) or flowchart for each procedure and work instruction. A PFD is a chart that graphically displays the progression of the steps in a process. Many people find it easier to follow a PFD than written instructions. While ISO 9000 does not specifically require the use of PFDs, some auditors like to see PFDs accompanying written procedures and sometimes will accept PFDs instead of written procedures.

Once the procedures and work instructions have been completed, they should be submitted to the manager of the department for approval. Policies should be approved by top management and by the managers of the departments affected.

A word of caution: When compiling procedures and work instructions, it is tempting to write them "as they should be done" to make the company's operation sound better to customers or the ISO auditor. An example of this would be saying that the company performs two inspections on each product when in practice there is only one inspection. This is not a good idea, because chances are the discrepancy will be caught by the auditor and the company will receive a nonconformance in this area.

Think About It...

Examine some of your company's SOPs and JWIs. Do they describe processes as they are actually done or as they should be done? If the latter, how should you go about changing them?

Document and Data Control

Even before the writing team begins the quality policy manual and documentation, the company needs to establish document control procedures. In fact, a major change to the 1994 ISO revision was the addition of the word "documented" 16 times. Document control (addressed in ISO 9001 Clause 4.5) is one of the ISO provisions with which companies have the most difficulty. A document control system has four major functions.

1. **To ensure that current versions of approved procedures and work instructions are available to everyone who needs them when and where they need them**—For example, a procedure or work instruction involving the use of a particular machine should be kept near that machine, not filed away in a cabinet to which the machine operator does not have access. Companies that issue quality manuals to individual employees generally "customize" the procedures and work instructions. That is, the employee receives only the SOPs and JWIs that affect his or her job. A production line worker

would receive (or have access to) SOPs and JWIs related to production but not those related to purchasing. A purchasing agent would not receive procedures and work instructions related to shipping.

2. **To ensure that any changes to existing quality documents are reviewed and approved**—Any changes to a document must be approved by the same functional authority who issued the original document. For example, if the director of manufacturing approved Procedure 4.9.1, any changes made to Procedure 4.9.1 must also be signed by the director of manufacturing.

3. **To ensure that all copies of obsolete documents (those that have been changed)are removed from circulation**—This is to ensure that the current version of any document that affects quality is available to everyone who needs it. To do this, ISO suggests a company establish a master list of all quality documents and who has them. This list must be maintained and updated so that no superseded document remains in circulation. These lists may be kept electronically, but those using the manuals must have access to them and must not be able to change them.

4. **To maintain and update the company's quality system**—While these provisions seem simple on the surface, enforcing them requires diligence and an eye for detail. In many companies, if a person is unsure of how to perform a certain job, it is common practice to just "run off a copy" of the established procedure and hand it out. In large companies, there may be hundreds of these unofficial copies in circulation. This can turn into a real problem if and when the procedure is changed. The person in charge of document control can replace the official copies but cannot replace the unofficial copies if he or she doesn't known how many exist and who has them. A person with an unofficial copy of the old procedure may follow it and create a product that does not meet the current quality standard or the needs of the customer.

Think About It...

What document control procedures does your company currently have in place? Are they sufficient to meet ISO 9000 requirements?

Standardizing and Writing SOPs and JWIs

Most companies that are just beginning the ISO process do not have standard procedures or work instructions. (As a matter of fact, most American companies with fewer than 2,000 employees and no military customers have no SOPs.) Even when procedures exist, there is considerable variation in how they are interpreted from department to department, or from shift to shift, or even from person to person. Procedures and work instructions must be made standard throughout the company before they are committed to writing.

Prioritize Functions for Standardization

Most companies will have dozens of procedures that must be standardized, and since they cannot all be done at once, the first step is to establish the order in which standardization will be done. The ISO/QS-9000 champion should determine which procedures and work instructions are used by the greatest number of people, which areas are most affected by nonstandard procedures or instructions, and which areas have a direct impact on quality as defined by the ISO standard to which the company will apply.

The first analysis can be conducted with a simple bar chart in which the bars, representing data, are arranged by height (frequency or importance). The highest bar (the most critical procedure) goes on the far left, with the others arranged in decreasing height (decreasing importance). Using this tool, it is easy to determine which procedures are used by the most people and, consequently, which have the greatest impact on the ISO process. (Figure 4.4 shows a bar chart displaying the number of people using certain procedures in a distribution company.) Do not write too many procedures. Use the guideline that a procedure is only needed when the absence of such could adversely affect quality. Remember, the auditor will hold you to any procedure you write.

The second analysis uses a statistical process control tool known as failure modes and effects analysis (FMEA). A FMEA measures the effect of the lack of standard procedures in a particular area. Each possible problem is listed, and values are assessed for their frequency and the negative effect they might have. Thus, the ISO champion can determine which areas are most affected by nonstandard procedures. FMEAs are required by QS-9000.

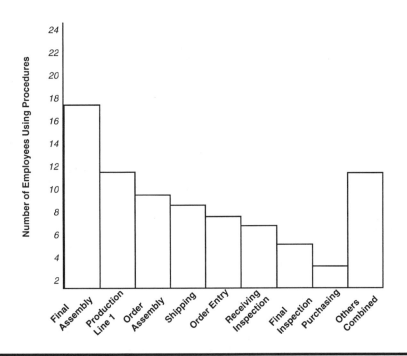

Figure 4.4 Use of Procedures Companywide

Internal Benchmarking

One of the best ways to standardize procedures and work instructions is through a process known as internal benchmarking. The ISO champion first interviews workers and supervisors to determine which person is considered to be the best at a certain task. (It is amazing how frequently consensus is reached on this person.) That individual then writes down the steps he or she follows to do that task. Other people who work in the same area review the steps and reach a consensus on the best way to perform this procedure. The procedure is then written as the SOP for that particular task. The ISO champion repeats this process for each procedure and work instruction.

Training

Once procedures and work instructions have been written and standardized, they must be taught to all employees. Because of the enormity of the task, the ISO champion will have to draw on the resources of the training department to ensure that the training is completed in a timely manner and does not disrupt operations too much.

A New Style of Training

For many companies, on-the-job training consists of having a new employee watch a veteran perform a task for a few hours—in some cases only a few minutes—and then pick up the rest of the job on his or her own. That level of training does not meet the intent of the ISO standards. ISO 9001 Clause 4.18 requires that training be sufficient to meet the requirements of the task. If, after completing the training, an employee cannot perform the task in the manner set out in the procedures or work instructions—without having to "pick it up on his or her own"—then the training does not comply with the intent of the standard. The ISO auditor is very likely to interview workers on the shop floor as to the type and amount of training they had for the job. If, in the auditor's opinion, the training was not adequate (generally evidenced by the fact that an employee is not using the prescribed procedure or is not following it correctly), the company will receive a nonconformance in this area.

The preferred method of training is to bring everyone who will be using the procedure to the training area and present the training. Two things are important here, particularly in a situation where 10 or 15 employees use the same procedure. The first is that the training must be presented professionally. The use of visual aids and hands-on experience with the process are highly recommended. The second point is that the trainer should use a person who is experienced in the process and who knows the job thoroughly as a co-trainer. This person is invaluable in answering all the "What if..." or "How do I do that if..." questions that will arise. A trainer, no matter how competent, is seldom prepared to answer questions that require intimate knowledge of the process. Also, don't forget to document the training; a sign-up sheet is a must for all training classes. If it is not documented, it did not happen.

ISO/Quality Training

In connection with on-the-job training in the new procedures, employees should receive training in basic quality principles, the elements of ISO/QS-9000, and how to be prepared for the audit. This training will help them understand why the company is pursuing ISO 9000 registration and should allay any fear or resentment at having to learn something new. It also should help them prepare for the changes ISO/QS will bring to the company and get ready for the registration audit. Training topics should include the following:

- An overview of ISO/QS-9000
- A brief description of each of the requirements of the standard to which the company is seeking registration (ISO 9001, 9002, or 9003 or QS-9000)
- How ISO registration will benefit the company—and them
- How ISO/QS will affect their jobs (usually jobs will become more structured)
- How they can help the company achieve registration
- What to expect from the audit
- An approximate time line for completing registration

This information can be delivered in several ways. One of the most effective methods is called monthly quality training. It consists of a series of 60- or 90-minute meetings with small groups (6 to 15 people) of employees in which a different quality topic is featured each month. The topic one month might be an overview of ISO 9000, while the next month's meetings might focus on standardizing processes.

As in other areas of ISO implementation, top management must take the lead in endorsing this training and stressing its importance. The training will be far more effective if employees know that the CEO is behind it and is also involved in the training—not just as an observer but as a participant.

The Internal Audit Process

Once the ISO/QS-9000 implementation process is underway, the company should start a series of internal audits. At first, as the ISO process is developing, the audits will be brief, informal looks at how implementation is proceeding. (This series of internal audits is required by ISO 9001 Clause 4.17). As ISO becomes more established in the company culture, the audits become more and more formal, culminating in a full-scale internal audit done shortly before the registration audit. (These formal internal audits must continue even after registration, to ensure that the company remains in compliance.)

An internal audit serves three purposes:

1. It allows a company to identify and correct any areas of nonconformance before the actual registration audit.
2. It can uncover areas that, although they may meet the requirements of the standard, can be improved to increase overall customer satisfaction.
3. It provides a "warm-up" to help employees prepare for the registration audit.

Scheduling Internal Audits

The first series of informal audits should be scheduled at random, although the departments to be audited should be given adequate time to prepare. The full-scale internal audits should be done when both the ISO champion and the department manager feel the department is ready. However, the department manager should not be allowed to put it off until there is insufficient time to make any required changes. Such action may make for some very unpleasant surprises when the registration audit is conducted.

The internal auditor should not be surprised to hear a department manager say, "Oh, you can come down and audit my department anytime," only to find a number of nonconformances. It sometimes takes an internal audit to "shock" a manager into the realization that ISO is not "business as usual."

It is not necessary that all departments be audited at the same time. In fact, in smaller companies, personnel constraints will require that the audits be staggered. Again, it is important that all areas of a company be audited in plenty of time to allow the results to be assessed and ensure that any necessary changes are made before the registration audit.

Internal Audit Guidelines

Internal audits are discussed fully in Chapter 6. However, the main guidelines bear a quick look:

1. **The internal audits should be made to seem as "real" as possible—** That is, the internal auditors should have a planned agenda and a checklist for compliance for each department. They should ex-

amine documentation and question workers for signs of noncompliance. This is not a game but a serious exercise with a real goal. The persons conducting the audit should not "take it easy" on people or departments. As a matter of fact, the internal auditors should be "tougher" than the external auditor.

2. **The audit should be as thorough as possible** —The internal auditors should examine every facet of every department and operation in the company that affects quality. This is the only way to ensure that all areas are in compliance with the standard. (*Note:* In most cases, the internal audit will be more wide-ranging than the actual registration audit; this is because internal auditors will have more time to conduct their examinations. This thoroughness is essential because while the ISO auditors will only audit a small portion—or "vertical slice"—of the company, they can choose that portion from anywhere within the firm.)

3. **The persons conducting the audit must be independent of the areas being audited** —In large companies, the audits will usually be conducted by members of the quality or audit department. In smaller companies, someone from purchasing may audit sales, while someone from shipping may audit production. This independence will ensure that nothing is covered up to keep a person or a department from looking bad. (There is always the chance of an unwritten gentlemen's agreement—"I'll protect yours if you protect mine." For this reason, the quality manager or ISO champion must carefully review the initial results of these internal audits.) Many registrars will accept an internal audit conducted by an outside consultant for small companies.

4. **The results of the audits should be given directly to both the department head and the CEO, along with the auditors' recommendations for changes**— Some department managers may refuse to accept the findings or approve changes. Getting the CEO involved will ensure that needed improvements are made. Again, the goal of these audits is to improve processes, not to find fault with individuals.

5. **Results of the audits, including departments audited, non-conformances noted, and any changes made as a result, should be included in the company's quality records, as required by ISO 9001 Clauses 4.16 and 4.17**—The ISO auditor will almost certainly ask to see records of internal audits.

Internal Audits for QS-9000

While the language of QS-9000 and ISO 9000 in relation to internal audits is nearly identical, QS-9000 comes with its own generic checklist for many of the requirements—the Quality System Assessment (QSA). This document should form the core for internal audits in companies seeking QS-9000. The questions that address specific procedures within the company are built around this core, as are additional questions that are required by the QS-9000 standard but not covered within the QSA instrument. The third-party registration firm will also use a version of the QSA; it is therefore important to prepare employees for the external audit by familiarizing them with these types of questions during the internal audit.

> **Think About It...**
>
> What procedures does your company have for conducting internal audits? Do they meet the intent of the ISO standards?

Follow-Up Activities

Any nonconformances found in the internal audit must be corrected. In many cases, this will involve only minor corrections—updating some documentation here or ensuring that equipment is calibrated there. Some areas, however, may require major effort to bring them into compliance with the intent of the standard. This is very common in sales and purchasing.

For example, the purchasing manager in one company had learned long ago that senior management believed that "the lowest price is the best deal." He had indoctrinated this belief into his four purchasing agents, who saw their mission as assuring that the price of any product or service was the lowest available, no matter what the quality. When the company decided to pursue registration to ISO 9000, the purchasing agents had a difficult time shifting from lowest price to lowest total cost, a concept that included quality, timeliness, durability, and other factors along with price. Even through the internal audit, the purchasing manager held out. Only when the results of the internal audit were brought to senior leadership did the purchasing manager change basic purchasing procedures and create an approved vendor list that was not based simply on lowest price.

The internal audits must be conducted early enough in the process to allow needed changes to be made. Functions where major nonconformances are found should be reaudited. These reaudits will not be full audits; they will cover only the areas where nonconformances were noted. If there is enough time before the registration audit, it is a good idea to hold a second (or even a third) full-scale internal audit.

The Pre-Audit

The pre-audit is exactly what the name implies—a "practice" audit conducted under actual audit conditions shortly before the registration visit. It is a company's final warm-up before the real thing. Generally, the pre-audit is conducted by the registrar. Many registration firms include a pre-audit in their fee structures; this should be determined when selecting a registrar. The pre-audit is conducted in exactly the same manner as the registration audit but in fewer days and with a reduced scope. A good showing here will bode well for the registration audit—if the company corrects any nonconformances noted. Although it is extremely unusual, it is not unheard of for a company to do so well on the pre-audit that the auditing firm will extend the scope and grant registration then and there.

If the registration firm does not schedule a pre-audit, the company should seek one from another outside source. It can be a customer, someone from a trade organization who has audit experience, or an ISO consultant.

The Registration Audit

Finally, it's time for the registration audit. The registration audit is covered in full in Chapter 7; however, a brief outline of the process is presented here. The audit starts when a company submits its quality manual (and sometimes, depending on the registrar, the procedures and work instructions as well) to the registration firm for review about two weeks prior to the scheduled visit. The auditors review the manual and decide which functions they are going to audit. The state of a company's quality manual also gives the auditors an idea of the state of its quality system. (Auditing firms have been known to cancel or postpone audits because a company's quality manual was in great disarray or simply not in compliance with the ISO standards.)

The Registration Visit

The auditing firm generally sends two auditors to perform the registration audit. At least one of the auditors will have experience in the type of business being audited or in-depth knowledge of the business. They ordinarily will spend one to five days at the company, with two to three days as the norm.

The auditors' first stop is usually the CEO's (general manager, plant manager, etc.) office. This is no mere courtesy call; management responsibility is the first requirement of ISO standards as well as QS-9000, and the auditors will want to assess the CEO's involvement in the quality process and particularly in ISO. The auditors will set out the agenda for the visit and then split up and proceed with the audit. They will stick to the agenda unless they find signs of nonconformance, in which case they will probe deeper into the problem area. They are accompanied by a company-designated "escort."

Once the audit is completed, the auditors will present an oral report of their findings. This report is soon followed by a written report. (Some registration firms present the written report at the conclusion of the audit.) The reports will include the finding in each area audited and list any nonconformances noted. They will also include the overall result of the audit.

Three Possible Results

There are three results are possible—pass, fail, or provisional. A provisional result is the most common. It means that while a company's quality system is generally in compliance with the standard, there are a few areas that need to be addressed before the company can be registered. If these discrepancies are not very serious, the company can attain registration simply by reporting to the registration firm the steps taken to address the discrepancies. If the nonconformances are serious, the registration firm may send the auditors back to the company to reinspect the area or areas where the discrepancies were noted. This is not a complete reaudit; only the areas where discrepancies were found will be reexamined. Once the nonconformances are resolved, the company is registered.

Further Action

While ISO registration is indeed something to celebrate, a company cannot afford to rest on its laurels. The auditors will return periodically for what are known as surveillance audits. These audits ensure that the company continues its process standardization, as well its record keeping, in accordance with the ISO standards. Companies have had their registrations revoked for failing a surveillance audit.

If other branches, sites, or plants are in the process of becoming registered, the ISO champion will want to share information from the audit with the other sites, especially the nonconformances the auditors cited. If these sites are following the same procedure that was declared nonconforming at the first site, they will be able to correct it before their registration audits.

Mining the ISO/QS-9000 Gold

Because ISO registration is highly valued by customers and potential customers and because QS-9000 is both required by certain customers and evidence of a high-quality companywide system, a company should take immediate steps to publicize its registration. This can be done in several ways. The most common is to add the registrar's stamp to all identity materials, including stationery, business cards, sales kits, and brochures. The company also should send press releases telling of its registration to local newspapers and to trade publications in its industry and the industries of its customers. If a company is the first in its area or the first in its industry to achieve registration, it should hold a press conference or make the CEO or ISO champion available for interviews with local newspapers or industry publications. The ISO champion could also write a case study of the company's ISO registration for an industry trade journal. It is also a good idea to hang a banner or sign announcing the registration in the lobby or outside the building.

Whatever methods are used, a company should definitely publish its registration. After all, most companies pursue ISO registration because of requests or pressure from customers. It therefore makes sense to tell these customers that the company has achieved registration. For most companies, the real "ISO gold" is the increased profitably that comes from implementing a comprehensive quality process, one that is customer oriented, proactive, and prevention based. Remember, both ISO and QS-9000 are means to an end, not the ends themselves.

Recap

In implementing ISO 9000, a company first must determine what functions should be included and if and how these functions or processes need to be altered to meet the intent of the standard. A company should decide on the content of the quality documentation system, and the ISO champion should write the policies, procedures and work instructions with input from those closest to the job. A company must implement a strict system of document control to ensure that current and accurate copies of all quality documents are available to people who need them. A company must conduct a series of internal audits to meet the requirements of ISO/QS-9000 and to help the firm prepare for the registration audit.

Chapter 5

Selecting a Registration Firm

Learning Objectives

By the end of this chapter, you should be able to:

- Define *scope, approach,* and *accreditation* as they apply to registration firms
- List three items that are included in the cost of the audit
- Enumerate three types of hidden costs that might be in a registrar's estimate
- List three skills a lead auditor should have other than technical training and experience

Introduction

The selection of a firm to perform the ISO/QS registration audit is one of the most important decisions a company will make in the ISO process. The registration firm will have a profound effect on the company seeking registration, not just during the audit itself but during the whole process, from preparation to registration. Each registration firm has a slightly different interpretation of or slant on the ISO requirements, and the

93

particular slant of the registration firm selected by a company will influence how the company sets up its system, writes its documentation, and performs the other tasks that are part of the preparation process. (This influence will be indirect; the audit firm will not tell a company how to prepare for the audit).

An auditing firm's philosophy will also be evident in its approach to the audit process itself. While registrars operating in the United States are thorough and diligent, some have reputations for being more stringent than others. Thus, the selection of a registrar is crucial to a company's ISO efforts and must be made fairly early in the ISO implementation process. The task is made both easier and more difficult by the recent proliferation of ISO registration firms in the United States. It is easier because with the increasing number of audit firms, a company is more likely to find a firm whose auditors have the background and experience necessary to conduct a meaningful audit of the company's operation. It is more difficult because of the confusion over exactly what industries each audit firm covers and which registrar's certification—or "mark"—is accepted where.

The Confusion Over Registration

The tremendous growth in demand for ISO registration has spawned a corresponding growth in registration firms in the United States and throughout the world. In 1991, there were about 12 firms offering ISO registration in the United States. By early 1993, there were at least 30 and by 1995, there were more than 70! This growth has created a somewhat chaotic situation. While all of these firms offer legitimate registration services, as of mid-1995, few were accredited to perform audits worldwide, and many registered firms in only one or two countries. Consequently, a company registered by a firm in its own country might find that the registration would not be accepted by a customer in another country. Much of this problem is due to the way the ISO regulations are set up.

The World Picture

The International Organization for Standardization created the ISO 9000 standards and has lobbied for their adoption worldwide. However, each country that adopts them is responsible for overseeing their administration and for overseeing the audit/registration process. Most countries have set up a quasi-governmental organization to oversee registration. For example, in the United Kingdom, one of the first countries to adopt the ISO 9000 guidelines, registration was established through what was once known as the National Accreditation Council of Certified Bodies, now known as the United Kingdom Accreditation Service (UKAS). That body was appointed by the British Department of Trade and Industry to accredit qualified auditing agencies, which would in turn register suppliers under the applicable ISO 9000 series standard. In the Netherlands, the governing body was established as the Raad voor de Certificate; it has been known since 1995 as RvA, in Italy it is Ente Nazionile Italiano di Unificazione.

In order to be accredited by the UKAS, auditing organizations have to comply with strict standards concerning the methods used to grant registration. Those criteria include issues such as how an accrediting agency recruits and selects its auditors, how it conducts the evaluations, how it measures its own level of performance, and how well it maintains its records. RvA and the other national bodies have similar but not exactly the same rules. It is these variations that cause the confusion over which registration is accepted in which country. Many countries accept certain registrations from other nations, but the cooperation is not universal. The confusion is especially acute in the case of companies that manufacture and sell products regulated by the European Community (EC) (building products, medical devices, toys, etc.); these companies must be registered by an acceptable registrar in order to place their goods on the market. In the case of nonregulated products, the acceptance of registration is based solely on market forces and customer opinion. (This discussion of worldwide registration is centered on actions in Europe because that is where the ISO 9000 process started. Japan and other Pacific Rim countries have since adopted the ISO 9000 series but, like the United States, their experiences have generally followed the European model.)

The U.S. Picture

In the United States, which was relatively late among major industrialized countries to board the ISO bandwagon, the picture is similarly confusing. Auditing to ISO 9000 began in the United States with a memorandum of understanding (MoU) between the British Standards Institute (BSi) and Underwriters Laboratories Inc. (UL), which had long performed both product and quality evaluations. Under that memorandum of understanding, BSi officially agreed to evaluate any ISO 9000 registration performed in the United States by UL and grant co-registration if the review was successful. As demand for registration grew, registrars from other countries established U.S. offices. In addition, some U.S. firms that performed audits for other purposes (the American Bureau of Shipping, for example) became certified by foreign national bodies to perform ISO audits as well.

In 1989, the American Society for Quality Control, a private entity widely considered an authority on quality assurance in the United States, established the Registrar Accreditation Board (RAB). The RAB joined with the American National Standards Institute, another private organization, to oversee registrations in the United States. Unlike similar bodies in other countries, the RAB had no official government endorsement, although it did sign MoUs for mutual recognition with some foreign national bodies.

In 1992, the U.S. government got into the act. Urged on by some industry leaders, the National Institute of Standards and Technology, an agency of the Department of Commerce, started the Conformity Assessment Systems Evaluation (CASE) program to oversee registrations for products intended for export to the EC. EC organizations, preferring to deal with government agencies, endorsed the CASE program. However, some industry leaders have resisted what they consider government intrusion into free enterprise. As of early 1997, this issue is still under review, and while there seems to be some progress toward common international recognition of registrars, it has been slow.

Criteria for Selecting a Registrar

As stated earlier, there are a growing number of firms that can provide ISO registration. These registrars range from companies with a long history of auditing, certification, and/or verification activities, such as Underwriters Laboratories and the American Bureau of Shipping, to more recent arrivals on the auditing scene, such as Quality System Registrars and AENOR (the Spanish national registration organization).

Today, more than ever, it is important to carefully select your registrar. Not all ISO auditors are qualified to grant QS-9000 registration. Not all auditors of QS-9000-approved registrars are themselves approved to conduct QS-9000 audits. As a safeguard, ask the potential registrars the questions in Table 5.1. Table 5.2 is a listing of all approved ISO 9000 registrars as of July 1, 1996. Registration firms will differ significantly in important areas, all of which need to be considered by a company shopping for a registrar. Some of these areas are:

- Scope
- Approach
- Accreditation
- Customer preference
- Cost

Table 5.1 Questions for Potential Registrars

1. **Registrar's scope and background**
   - Experience in ISO auditing in the United States
   - Audit experience in your industry
   - Auditor qualifications
   - Auditor predictability over time—percentage who stay with auditee

2. **Quality system implementation philosophy**
   - Required system maturity for initial audit
   - Documentation requirements
   - Specifically: "How long must the system have been operational to pass the audit?"

3. **Criteria for passing the audit**
   - Majors versus minors/Category 1 versus Category 2
   - Grading system
   - Percentage of auditees that have passed initial audit with/without pre-audit

4. **Specific costs for corporate and branches/remote sites**
   - Review of proposal
   - Anticipated costs for other sites

5. **Auditor's mark**
   - Where the mark is held
   - If there are MoUs, and if so, with whom?
   - Plans for additional recognition

6. **Policy re surveillance audits**
   - How often
   - Scheduled/not scheduled
   - Scope

7. **Remediation of nonconformances—criteria**

8. **Other**

Table 5.2 Accredited Registrars Operating in the United States as of July 1, 1996

The registrars meet one of two criteria:
- They are accredited to issue ISO 9000 certificates by an accrediting organization
- They have an agreement with another accredited firm to mutually recognize ISO 9000 certificates

Registrar Performing Assessments	Acronym
ABS Quality Evaluations, Inc.	ABS QE
A.G.A. Quality, A Service of International Approval Services	A.G.A.
AIB Registration Services	AIBRS
AIB-Vincotte AV Qualite	AV Qualite
American Association for Laboratory Accreditation	A2LA
American Quality Assessors	AQA
The American Society of Mechanical Engineers	ASME
ASCERT USA, Inc.	ASCERT
Asociacion Espanola de Normalizacion y Certificacion	AENOR
Associated Offices Quality Certification	AOQC
Bellcore Quality Registration	BQR
British Standards Institution Quality Assurance	BSI QA
Bureau Veritas Quality Internatl (N America, Inc)	BVQI
Canadian General Standards Board	CGSB
Centerior Registration Services	CRS
Ceramic Industry Certification Scheme, Ltd.	CICS
CGA Approvals–Canadian Operations of International Approval Services (IAS)	CGA
Defense Electronics Supply Center	DESC
Det Norske Veritas	DNV
DLS Quality Technology Associates, Inc.	DLS
Davy Registrar Services, Inc.	DRS
EAGLE Registrations, Inc.	EAGLE
Electronic Industries Quality Registry	EQR
Entela, Inc., Quality System Registration Div.	ENTELA
Factory Mutual Research Corporation	FMRC
GBJD Registrars Limited	GBJD
German Association for the Certification of Quality Management Systems	DQS
Global Registrars, Inc.	GRI
Hartford Steam Boiler Inspection & In Co.	HSB
Instituto Mexicano de Normalizacion y Certificacion A.C.	IMNC
International Certifications, Ltd.	ICL
Intertek Services Corporation	INTERTEK
ISOQAR	ISOQAR

Registrar Performing Assessments	Acronym
KEMA Register Quality, Inc.	KEMA
Kemper Registrar Services, Inc.	KRS
KPMG Quality Registrar	KPMG QR
Litton Systems Canada Ltd, Quality System Registrars	LSL QSR
Lloyd's Register Quality Assurance Limited	LRQA
The Loss Prevention Certification Board Limited	LPCB
National Quality Assurance, Ltd.	NQA
National Standards Authority of Ireland	NSAI
NSF International	NSF
OMNEX-Automotive Quality Systems Registrar	OMNEX-AQSR
OTS Quality Registrars, Inc.	OTSQR
Performance Review Institute	PRI
Perry Johnson Registrars, Inc.	PJR
Professional, Environmental Caring Services QA, Ltd.	PECS
Quality Assurance Association of France	AFAQ
Quality Certification Bureau, Inc.	QCB
Quality Management Institute	QMI
Quality Systems Assessment Registrar	QUASAR
Quality Systems Registrars, Inc.	QSR
Quebec Quality Certification Group	GQCQ
Raytheon Quality Registrar, Inc.	RQR
Scott Quality Systems Registrars, Inc.	SQSR
SGS International Certification Services, Inc.	SGS ICS
SGS International Certification Services Canada, Inc.	SGS ICS Canada
Sira Certification Service/Sira Test & Certification Ltd.	SCS
Smithers Quality Assessments, Inc.	SQA
Steel Related Industries Quality System Registrars	SRI
TRA Certification, A Division of TR Arnold and Associates, Inc.	TRA-CD
TUV America and TUV Product Service	TUV AMERICA & TUV PS
TUV ESSEN	TUV ESSEN
TUV Rheinland of North America, Inc.	TUV RHEINLAND
Underwriters Laboratories Inc.	UL
Underwriters Laboratories of Canada	UL of Canada
United Registrar of Systems, Ltd.	URS
Vehicle Certification Agency	VCA
Warnock Hersey Professional Services, Ltd.	WH

Scope

Scope is a critically important concept to understand in selecting an auditing firm. It essentially refers to the competencies of an auditing firm and the experiences of its auditors. For example, the following are three scope statements from ISO registration firms operating in the United States:

1. TUV Rheinland: "In North America, TUV Rheinland specializes in auditing the following industries: automotive; electronic; industrial; medical; pressure vessels and related."
2. Lloyd's Register Quality Assurance Ltd. (LRQA): "LRQA's policy is to apply for accreditation in every new business it undertakes. LRQA offers a complete range of accredited services in architecture; civil engineering; consumer services; design; electrical appliances; electronic components; fabrication; food and drink producers, packagers and distributors; installation of fixtures and fittings; lighting equipment; metallurgical; project management; steelwork erection; switchgear; telecommunications; textile dyes and pigments.
3. ABS Quality Evaluations (QE): "ABS QE is accredited to certify in many industries, including: electrical equipment; engines and gears, industrial machinery, marine and offshore products, pressure vessels; ship management companies; structural and mechanical metal products."

Define Scope Accurately

There are, of course, many similarities among these statements of scope, as there are among those of other ISO registration firms. (Table 5.3 shows a sample of registration firms [28 out of the 70] accredited to do ISO registration in the United States, along with their scopes.) Scope is important because the auditors must understand a company's industry in order to understand its quality system. As the push for ISO registration expands beyond manufacturing and into the service sector (and soon, even into retail), it will become even more important for a company to define the scope for its audit capabilities and to define this scope as accurately as possible.

For example, a company specializing in the manufacture of precision valves, commodity chemicals, or piston rings will likely not have a problem with scope for an audit; there are many auditors from which to

Selecting a Registration Firm

Table 5.3 Quality Registrars

Registrar	Phone/Contact	Scope
ABS Quality Evaluations (ABS QE) 263 North Belt East Houston, TX 77060	(713) 873-9400 Patti Wigginton	Electrical equipment, engines and gears, industrial machinery, marine and offshore products, pressure vessels, ship management companies, structural and mechanical metal products
Asociacion Espanola de Normalizacion y Certificacion (AENOR) Fernandez de la Hoz, 52 28010 Madrid Spain	34 14 10 4851 Isabel Ramirez	AENOR is a third-party registering body performing multisectorial activities
American Association for Laboratory Accreditation (A2LA) 656 Quince Orchard Rd., #356 Gaithersburg, MD 20878-1409	(301) 670-1377 Peter Unger	Laboratory accreditation services for virtually all types of tests; registration services for environmental reference materials suppliers
A.G.A. Quality (Division of A.G.A. Laboratories) 8501 E. Pleasant Valley Road Cleveland, OH 44131	(216) 524-4990	Aerospace, business, professional services, chemicals, distribution, electrical, electromechanical products, mechanical products and processes, nuclear, printing, publishing, test laboratories
British Standards Institution Quality Assurance (BSi) P.O. Box 375 Milton Keynes MK14 6LL United Kingdom	0908-220-908 Business Development Enquiries	The accredited scope of BSi's quality assurance registration program covers almost every standard industry classification
Bureau Veritas Quality International Inc. (BVQI) North American Central Office 509 North Main Street Jamestown, NY 14701	(716) 484-9002 Greg Swan	BVQI has a comprehensive scope in most major manufacturing and service areas; BVQI's control system has been designed to meet the requirements of European Norm (EN) 45012 and ISO 9001

Table 5.3 Quality Registrars (continued)

Registrar	Phone/Contact	Scope
Ceramic Industry Certification Scheme LTD. (CICS) Queens Road Penkhull Stoke-on-Trent ST4 7LQ United Kingdom	(44) 782-41-1008 J.E. Leake	Most types of ceramics and related industries, including bathroom sanitaryware; bricks, roofing tiles, and pavers; ceramic transfers; floor and wall tiles; raw materials and equipment suppliers to the ceramics industry; refractory and industrial ceramics; tableware; whiteware; colors, frits, and glazes; clays
Det Norske Veritas Industry, Inc. (DNVI) 16340 Park Ten Place, Suite 100 Houston, TX 77084	(713) 579-9003 Steve Cummings	Almost all industries, including chemical processing, electronics and instrumentation, and manufacture of oilfield equipment
ENTELA Laboratories, Inc. 3033 Madison Avenue SE Grand Rapids, MI 49548	(616) 247-0515 (800) 55-TESTS Paul Riksen/ Robert Kosack	ENTELA Laboratories has a comprehensive scope in most manufacturing and several service areas; ENTELA's control system has been designed to meet the requirements of ISO 9001 and EN 45012
French Association for Quality Assurance (AFAQ) Tour Septentrion Cedex 9 92018 Paris La Defense France	(33) (1) 47 73 49 49 Sylvie Rolland	Works in connection with European standard EN 45012; works with a wide range of industries; no specialization
Intertek Services Corporation 9900 Main Street, Suite 500 Fairfax, VA 22031	(703) 476-9000 Frederick J. Becker	Aerospace, chemical processing, computers, electrical and electromechanical, electronics and microelectronics, general manufacturing, pharmaceuticals, telecommunications, machinery and equipment
KEMA-USA, Inc. (KEMA) 4379 County Line Road Chalfont, PA 18914	(215) 822-4281 Theo Stoop	KEMA assesses quality management standards according to ISO 9000 series and other standards

Selecting a Registration Firm 103

Lloyd's Register Quality Assurance LTD. (LRQA) 33-41 Newark Street Hoboken, NJ 07030	(201) 963-1111 David Hadlet	Architecture; civil engineering; consumer services; design; electrical appliances; electronic components; fabrication; food and drink producers, packagers, and distributors; installation of fixtures and fittings; lighting equipment; metallurgical; project management; steelwork erection; switchgear; telecommunications; textile dyes and pigments
Loss Prevention Certification Board LTD. (LPCB) Melrose Avenue Borehamwood Hertfordshire WD6 2BJ United Kingdom	44-081-207-2345 Chris Beedel	LPCB's scope comprises firms that provide fire protection and security products, systems, and services
MET Laboratories, Inc. 914 W. Patapsco Avenue Baltimore, MD 21230-3432	(410) 354-3300 Joyce Holton	Using ISO 9000 as a basis, MET conducts unannounced inspection of a manufacturer's facility to assure continuing compliance; MET certifies that the manufacturing process complies with ISO 9002 for the product certified
National Quality Assurance, LTD. (NQA) 1146 Massachusetts Avenue Boxborough, MA 01719	(508) 635-9256 James P. O'Neil	Building engineering services; heating elements; domestic appliance servicing; electroplating; cutting tools; general process instrumentation; radio, telecommunications, and data systems; packing and blending of raw materials, synthetics, and foodstuffs; water pumps and associated controls; provision of catering systems
National Standards Authority of Ireland (NSAI) North American Certification Services 5 Medallion Center (Greeley Street) Merrimack, NH 03054	(603) 424-7070 Richard Berrier	The Irish national standards board, ASAI provides certification to all products and services.

Table 5.3 Quality Registrars (continued)

Registrar	Phone/Contact	Scope
NSF International 3475 Plymouth Road P.O. Box 130140 Ann Arbor, MI 48113-0140	(313) 769-8010 Garry Puglio	NSF is an independent, private, nonprofit organization providing third-party services through programs that focus on public health and environmental quality
Quality Management Institute (QMI) Suite 800, Mississauga Executive Center Two Robert Speck Parkway Mississauga, Ontario, Canada L4Z 1H8	(416) 272-3920 Catherine Neville	QMI's applicants are from across major industry segments, including telecommunications, petrochemicals, chemicals, electrical and electronics, pulp and paper, mechanical, mining, and the service sector
Quality Systems Registrars, Inc. (QSR) 1555 Naperville/Wheaton Road Suite 206 Naperville, IL 60563	(708) 778-0120 Richard Kleckner	Air transportation, chemicals/allied products, computer equipment, electrical/electronic equipment and components, engineering, accounting, research; fabricated metal products, industrial/commercial machinery, lumber/wood products, measuring/analyzing/controlling instruments, mining/quarrying, oil/gas extraction, paper, petroleum refining, pharmaceuticals, photographic/medical/optical goods, pipelines (except natural gas), primary metal industries, rubber/plastic products, textiles, transportation equipment, wholesale trade
SGS Standards Approval and Compliance, Inc. (SGS Canada) 90 Gough Road Markham, Ontario, Canada L3R 5V5	(416) 479-1160 Raymond Grayson	Building, chemicals, distribution, electronics/electrical, engineering, foodstuffs, plastics/rubber, stockholding, textiles, wood/paper
SGS Yarsley Quality Assured Firms (SGS Yarsley) 1415 Park Avenue Hoboken, NJ 07030	(201) 792-2400 Emani Pires	Building, chemicals, distribution, electronics/electrical, engineering, foodstuffs, plastics/rubber, stockholding, textiles, wood/paper

SIRA Certification Service/SIRA Test & Certification Limited (SCS) Saighton La. Saighton Chester CH 36EG United Kingdom	(0244) 332200 Graham Tortoishell	SCS is accredited to certify electrical and electronic equipment, including that for potentially explosive atmospheres, the product conformity certification scope of accreditation includes similar types of equipment
Steel Related Industries Quality System Registrar (SRI) 2000 Corporate Drive, Suite 450 Wexford, PA 15090	(412) 935-2844 Dr. Peter B. Lake James H. Bytnar	Mining/quarrying, chemicals, primary metals, stone/clay/glass, fabricated metal products, industrial machinery/equipment, motor vehicles/equipment, transportation/warehousing, research/management services, engineering/conduction services, laboratory apparatus/instruments
TUV America (TUV) 5 Cherry Hill Drive Danvers, MA 01923	(508) 777-7999 Manfred Popp/ Mark Alpert	Steam boilers/pressure vessels, nuclear power plants, refineries/pipelines, industrial machinery, subway systems, electrical equipment, control equipment/computers, medical equipment, automotive equipment, amusement park rides
TUV Rheinland of North America, Inc. (TUV Rheinland) 12 Commerce Road Newtown, CT 06470	(203) 426-0888 Joseph DeCarlo	Automotive, electronic, industrial, medical, pressure vessel and related
Underwriters Laboratories, Inc. (UL) 1285 Walt Whitman Road Melville, NY 11747-3081	(516) 271-6200 ext. 837 Robert Zott	Chemicals, information technology equipment, electronic equipment, fabricated metal products, industrial/commercial machinery, measuring/analyzing/controlling instruments, paper, pipelines (except natural gas), wholesale trade/durable goods industries

Table 5.3 Quality Registrars (continued)

Registrar	Phone/Contact	Scope
Vincotte USA, Inc. (AV) 10497 Town & Country Way Suite 900 Houston, TX 77024	(713) 465-2850 Terry Heaps	Advanced technology systems, calibration of test/measuring equipment, chemical manufacturing, chemical/mechanical/electrical testing, civil engineering projects, food, industrial projects, information technology, medical devices, nondestructive testing, nuclear safety, petrochemical equipment, power generation

Selecting a Registration Firm **107**

choose, and they will all have the necessary scope. A company that manufactures electronic gear, for example, could select any number of the firms listed in Table 5.2. However, for companies that distribute electrical components, move chemical and petrochemical products along the intracoastal waterway, produce refractory ceramics, or manufacture a highly sophisticated and highly proprietary component used in propulsion systems, scope could be a major factor in choosing an auditing firm. Scope could also be a problem for a company that has two separate operations (e.g., valve manufacture and valve repair) under the same roof. Companies in these and similar situations need to be very careful in examining the scopes of potential auditors. In examining a potential registrar's scope, a company should ask for the names of companies the registrar has audited, especially firms in the company's own industry. This will give the company an idea of the areas in which the auditing firm has experience.

A company that has undergone audits for other quality standards and that has established a relationship with an auditing firm may do well to select that auditor to do its ISO assessment. For example, a marine transportation company may select ABS, or a manufacturer of electrical appliance may select Underwriters Laboratories simply because they are familiar with those auditors' scopes, and those auditors know the companies' operations.

Examine the Individual Auditor's Scope

The qualifications and experience of the auditor who actually does the audit are also critical factors. The number of registered companies in the United States has grown from 100 in 1991 to 500 in 1992 to over 10,000 by mid-1996. In order to handle this explosion of demand for registrars, many firms have been hiring auditors at a rapid rate, sometimes as often as one a week. While many of these recent hires have been auditors for some time, have a strong auditing background, and may even have achieved the status of certified quality auditor, some will not have this background.

While the registration firm may not be able to identify the auditor who will perform the actual assessment at this early stage, a company has the right to and should ask to examine the auditing credentials of potential auditors. A company should look for the training the auditor has had, experience both as an auditor and before, and the companies which he or she has audited. Many auditors have technical degrees. A company should determine whether or not the technical degree qualifies the auditor to assess its operation. Does an electrical engineer have the background to properly evaluate a large distribution company or an accounting firm? (The qualifications necessary to become an ISO auditor are covered fully below.) While it is rarely done, a company does have the right to reject a potential auditor if he or she does not possess adequate credentials in terms of training and experience to conduct the company's audit. Of course, if it is a QS-9000 audit, the auditor will need to present proof that he or she is certified to conduct this QS-9000 audit.

Think About It...

Examine the scope of the registrars listed in Table 5.3. Based solely on scope, which of these registrars would you select for your company?

Approach

The registrar's approach is almost as important as its scope. Approach refers to how the company conducts the audit. Some registrars conduct the audit strictly by the applicable ISO 9001 or 9002 paragraph (e.g., one auditor would check document control procedures in each department [Clause 4.5], while another would examine purchasing procedures [Clause 4.6]). Others conduct audits strictly by department (e.g., one auditor would examine production, checking for compliance with all applicable requirements, while another assessed purchasing, also checking for compliance with all applicable requirements). Still others use a combination of the two methods, while some vary their approach to fit the operation of the individual company.

The method the registrar uses for conducting the audit will probably have no effect on the findings or the final outcome. However, the method could have an effect on how a company sets up its documentation system and how it prepares for the audit. Therefore, approach is an important factor.

Nonconformances

Part of a registrar's approach involves how it deals with any nonconformances it may uncover. Different registrars and, frankly, even different auditors within the same registration firm may rate non-conformances differently (as major or minor), and they may differ in the number of nonconformances they will allow before denying registration. Some registrars, for example, will deny registration because of one major nonconformance (although they will generally give the company a provisional mark for the audit and grant registration when the nonconformance is remedied). Others have been known to allow more major nonconformances (although their definition of a major nonconformance may be narrower than that of other registrars). Over the years, due to the influence of the RAB, the UKAS, and the RvA, these differences have become less pronounced.

During one witnessed audit, an auditor of one of the most well-known registration firms in the United States told the company's management representative, "I realize these four nonconformances might be considered minor, but I want management's attention, so I am calling them major."

Because the number and type of nonconformances uncovered will determine whether a company passes or fails the audit, a company needs to get firm, clear answers from the auditing firm on its nonconformance policy. How many major and/or minor nonconformances does it take to fail the audit? How many major and/or minor nonconformances is a company allowed to have and still be granted provisional registration, pending corrective action? How many minor nonconformances in one area does it take to constitute a major nonconformance?

To get these answers, a company should consider developing a number of hypothetical scenarios covering some areas of its operation and ask the auditing firm whether it would assess a major or minor nonconformance (or no nonconformance) in each case. While some registrars may be uncomfortable providing a reply to a hypothetical question, the question may provide the auditor an opportunity to explain the registrar's particular system in more detail. The following are a few sample scenarios:

- One worker in a particular area does not follow written work instructions in performing a task, while everyone else who performs that task does follow the written procedures. Major, minor, or none?

- Evidence indicates that contracts were not reviewed as they should have been (there are no verifying signatures), but the contracts were repeat orders involving long-standing specifications. Major, minor, or none?

- The contracts mentioned above bear signatures indicating review but have no dates indicating when they were reviewed. Major, minor, or none?
- Several revised company procedures bear signatures that are different from those on the original procedure, possibly indicating that the authority for the revision is not the same as the originating authority. Major, minor, or none?

Think About It...

Consider each of the sample scenarios. If you were the auditor, would you assess a major nonconformance, a minor nonconformance, or none?

Most registrars provide a company representative with a written report detailing the nonconformance and the evidence for it at the time the nonconformance is uncovered. This policy is not universal however, so a company should ask what the registrar's policy is. It also makes sense for a company seeking registration and waiting to know more about the audit process to obtain ISO 10011-1, Guidelines for Auditing Quality Systems—Part 1: Auditing.

Accreditation

As stated earlier, there is no universal system for certifying auditors or recognizing registration outside the home country of a particular registrar. Therefore, a company must determine exactly what registration by a particular registrar means. For example, registration by the British Standards Institute is recognized in most countries where ISO 9000 has been adopted, while registration by "Joe's ISO Audits in a Flash" may not be recognized by anyone other than Joe himself. While few choices are that cut-and-dried, a company does need to check how widely a registrar's mark is accepted.

Most U.S. registrars have a memorandum of understanding (MoU) with one or more internationally recognized accreditation bodies. The UKAS (United Kingdom) and RvA (The Netherlands) are the two most widely known and widely recognized. A MoU means that a U.S. registrar agrees to abide by certain standards in training and qualifying auditors, in conducting audits, and in keeping records. In turn, the UKAS and/or RvA agree to recognize and accept any registrations granted by this registrar. In many cases, other countries' accrediting bodies also will accept the registrations, because they have been recognized by the UKAS and RvA. (A company may have to pay an extra fee to have its name put on the list of registered companies in each country.) Today, MoUs are becoming less common as cooperation increases among these governing bodies.

Once a U.S. system of registration becomes fully operational, a company will be able to get accreditation information on registrars from the U.S. accreditation body. Until that happens, however, a company should ask a potential registrar to outline its means for establishing competence. Questions a company should ask include the following:

- With which EC registration bodies does the company have MoUs? Is the company's registration automatically accepted by those bodies, or does the company have to make separate application to those bodies? Does the company have to pay an extra fee to be listed by those bodies?
- If the accreditation body does not represent an EC member state, is that state seeking EC membership or is the body seeking to become registered by the EC? If so, when will it be recognized?
- Has the accreditation body adopted the EN 45012 standard (an internationally recognized standard covering quality system registration)? If not, is it planning to do so? When?
- Does the registrar subcontract any activities to another person or organization (an independent auditor, for example)? If so, is this person or organization recognized by an accreditation body of an EC state?

When interviewing the auditor about scope, qualifications, and approach, the questions in Table 5.1 are recommended.

Customer Preference

Many companies that implement ISO/QS-9000 registration programs do so because of pressure from customers. Therefore, it makes sense for a company to ask its customers if they have any recommendations concerning ISO registrars. Many customers will have no preference; they care only that the company has a quality system that is sufficiently standardized to earn registration. However, some customers will have a definite recommendation (in some cases a requirement) concerning the registrar a company uses. For example, a petrochemical company in the Southwest will recognize supplier registrations by only three registration firms. It gives its suppliers a choice of those three, but it won't accept any others. Other companies may have similar requirements.

Several reasons exist for such preferences. The main reason is that all registrars are not created equal. Some registrars have reputations for being tough—they audit a company very carefully and are very exacting (some auditees might say picky) in their interpretations of the standards and their definitions of compliance with those standards. A company registered by one of these firms is considered to have its quality system in place and is considered to be a model supplier. Other registrars have reputations for being "easy"; they are more lax in their interpretations of the standards and may allow a company to get by with less than 100 percent compliance. (In one instance, an "approved" policy manual was provided as evidence of ISO readiness. The approval had been granted by one of the largest registrars in the United States, yet the policy manual itself was typewritten with several phrases deleted. Most registrars would not have accepted this manual as evidence of a fully functioning quality system.)

However, whether or not these reputations are valid is not important. The important thing is that many customers do have perceptions of differences among auditing and judge potential suppliers by the reputation of their registrars. Unfortunately for suppliers, these reputations are not universal; a registrar considered tough by one customer may be considered easy by another. A company must ask its customers for recommendations.

Sometimes, customers will recommend that a supplier be audited by the same registrar that audited the customer. The customer knows how that registrar conducts audits and understands how it assesses compliance with the standards. In other words, the customer knows what it is getting when a supplier is registered by the same registrar.

Occasionally, a company may find itself in a situation where one major customer insists that the registration audit be performed by a particular registrar—and will accept no other—and another major customer makes the same demand—but for a different registrar. The company should try to negotiate a compromise with the two customers. If neither will budge and the company does not want to lose either of them, it may have to seek dual registration. If that happens (and it has, although it is very rare), the company should ask one of the registrars if it will accept the other registrar's findings and issue a second registration (for an additional fee, of course). Otherwise, the company will have to undergo an entire second audit.

Think About It...

Is your company implementing ISO because of pressure from a customer? If so, has that company expressed a recommendation for a particular registrar? If so, do you know why?

Cost

The cost of an ISO or QS-9000 assessment will depend on many factors, including the number of employees a company has, the number and nature of its processes, and the number of sites to be included in the audit. It is almost impossible to provide a blanket figure, or even a range, that will apply to all companies. It is a sure bet, however, that registration will cost even the smallest company at least $5,000, and costs could be as high as $200,000 for a large multisite, multiyear audit process.

After identifying several possible registrars based on scope, a company should get estimates from each of them. Costs can vary widely from registrar to registrar. For example, a distribution company with 14 small branches received estimates ranging from $46,000 to $113,000 from five registrars, all of which had essentially the same per diem costs. These costs include the following:

- The application fee
- Preparation on the part of the auditing firm
- Time spent reviewing the company's quality manual
- The pre-assessment meeting and/or pre-audit (including the length of the meeting and the number of auditors sent)
- Auditor days involved in the audit (a very small company may only have one auditor for one day, whereas a very large site might require four auditors for four days; the average is two auditors for two to three days. Charges today typically run from $1,100 to $1,500 per auditor per day.)
- The auditors' expenses (transportation, lodging, and meals)
- Time spent compiling the final report

- Time spent reviewing corrective action by the company to remedy nonconformances
- Travel time (some registrars charge travel time, and others do not)

When reviewing an audit firm's estimate, a company should be aware of possible hidden costs. For example, after a company is registered, the audit firm will return every six months or so for surveillance visits. Some companies include the cost of these surveillance visits in their estimates; others do not. A company should ask the registrar if these costs are included in the estimate because the company will have to undergo five or six surveillance visits during the three years the registration is in effect. The company should be sure to get the total long-term costs for these visits. Other questions a company should ask include the following:

- If the company has to postpone the audit, will it have to pay cancellation charges? How much time before the audit (four weeks, six weeks) do cancellation charges apply? How much will they be? What if the registrar postpones the audit because it feels the company is not ready?
- Will the auditor's time be billed by the hour, by the day, or at a flat rate for the audit? Is the company billed extra if the auditor decides to extend the audit to investigate a particular area further?
- Will the company be charged extra if the auditor has to make a return visit to verify the effectiveness of corrective action?
- If surveillance visits are extra: How many will there be over the life of the registration? How long will each take? What parts of the quality system will be checked during each visit? What is the approximate cost for a surveillance visit?
- When the original registration expires, what will the reassessment cost? Will it cost the same as the original audit? Will it take as long as the original audit?
- Does the company have to pay for the auditors' travel time? If so, are the auditors located at the registrar's headquarters, or do they have to travel farther?
- If a company has multiple sites: Will the costs for auditing additional sites be the same as for auditing the main facility? What if the sites are audited one after the other by the same team?

Once a company has examined estimates from all potential auditors, it should consider the factors covered above to determine which registrar provides the best combination of scope, approach, accreditation, customer recommendations, reputation, and price. Is a company really saving money on a less costly registrar if that firm's mark is not accepted in as many places or by as many customers as the mark of another registrar that submitted a higher estimate? If the first registrar does not have auditors who can accurately assess the company's quality system, is this really a savings?

Auditor Qualifications

The growth of ISO and QS-9000 registration has caused a corresponding growth in the number of people conducting ISO audits. Where the community of auditors once was fairly small and close-knit, it now has thousands of new members. Most of these new auditors have the training and background necessary to perform quality system audits, at least in certain industries. But not all of them do, and a company selecting a registration firm must be able to assess if that firm's auditors are qualified.

Auditor Certification

Many ISO auditors in the United States are certified through the United Kingdom's UKAS. Most of these certifications are also recognized by the RAB, the U.S. registration supervisory organization. The UKAS has devised a National Registration Scheme for Assessors of Quality Systems, which outlines the qualifications lead auditors and auditors must have before they can perform ISO 9000 audits. Certification as an auditor is based on a point system in which potential auditors are awarded points for education in a technical discipline, work experience, quality assurance experience, and auditing experience. (This system is too involved to be covered here. Those who want to learn more about the registration scheme should contact the UKAS and/or obtain ISO 10111-2, Guidelines for Auditing Quality Systems—Part 2, Qualification Criteria for Auditors.)

The auditor must also undergo a rigorous training course approved by the International Register of Certified Auditors or the RAB and taught under license by numerous U.S. firms. This week-long course, which typically requires a great deal of extracurricular study and work to pass (some training firms are more rigorous in their presentation of the course than others), covers the duties of an auditor; interpretation of the requirements of ISO 9001, 9002, and 9003; and general audit procedures. It also involves a number of simulations of audit situations. The number of such courses has multiplied. In 1991, just a handful of lead auditor certification courses were held in the United States. In the last six months of 1996 alone, over 150 such courses were held throughout the United States.

A person who passes this course, including a written examination, is considered a certified ISO auditor (if he or she has the necessary background and experience cited above). An auditor can become a lead auditor by participating in a specified number of ISO audits (usually 10, although sometimes registration firms require that an auditor participate in as many as 20 audits before being sent out as a lead auditor, especially in an industry where the auditor has little or no work experience).

Although ISO registration is still relatively new to the United States, auditing to other standards (such as MIL-Q-9858A, the Nuclear Regulatory Commission's 10CFR50, Specification Q-1 of the American Petroleum Institute, the American Society of Mechanical Engineers' NQA-1, 1989, and others) is not. The American Society for Quality Control has a certified quality auditor program, and both the nuclear industry and the American Petroleum Institute certify auditors in those disciplines. There are others as well, most notably the Institute for Quality Assurance, a British organization. Many U.S. ISO auditors held one or more of these certifications before they became involved in ISO. A company shopping for a registrar should ask for all of the qualifications of the auditors that will be performing the assessment. Again, this is particularly true in a QS-9000 audit.

Not all ISO auditors are approved as QS-9000 auditors. Approval for a QS-9000 auditor is not automatic, even if the auditor's registration company has QS-9000 approval. QS-9000 has established a second set of auditor qualifications for QS-9000 audits and, indeed, these audits are different and more wide ranging and demanding than the basic ISO 9000 audit.

Other Lead Auditor Skills

Although certification covers only an auditor's training and experience, a good lead auditor must have skills beyond the technical sphere. He or she also must be an excellent communicator, a good organizer, and a strong but flexible leader. The technical training and background allow the lead auditor to assess a company's quality system; the other skills allow the auditor to work with a company's—and his or her own—people.

Communication Skills

From the point of view of a company being audited, the lead auditor *is* the registration firm and, by extension, ISO or QS-9000 itself. He or she is the one who sets up the audit, conducts meetings with the auditee, and tells the auditee the outcome of the audit process. The lead auditor also conducts interviews with company employees, including the CEO. Therefore, he or she must be able to communicate facts about the audit to people from all types of backgrounds. The lead auditor must be able to put people at ease during an interview and ask questions that will elicit the response he or she wants, even if the subject is nervous or reluctant to talk.

The lead auditor also must have diplomatic ability. Many companies may resent the concept of an audit and the auditors who perform it, especially if the auditors find a number of nonconformances. Company representatives may become argumentative if the findings of the audit reflect poorly on the company. The lead auditor must be able to defuse these feelings while insisting that the audit results be heeded. He or she must not become flustered or resentful when the auditee questions his or her findings.

Organizational Skills

The lead auditor is the person who puts together the format for the audit. He or she sets the agenda with representatives of the auditee, decides what areas of the company will be audited in what manner, and oversees the preparation of the checklists by which the audit will be conducted. It is essential, therefore, that the lead auditor be able to organize projects well, in a way that outsiders can understand. In many cases, lead auditors perform a different audit each week, while handling the early or closing stages of other audits. They must be able to handle multiple projects on tight deadlines.

Leadership Skills

The lead auditor generally selects the other auditors who will assist in the audit. He or she must be able to select members according to their ability to conduct an assessment and their ability to work as a team and must provide guidance to all the auditors working with him or her, especially those who are newcomers. Above all, the lead auditor must have the ability to skillfully mediate any disputes or differences of opinion that arise among the members of the audit team.

Think About It...

Judging by the information on auditors' qualifications and skills, can you identify anyone in your company who would make a good ISO auditor, with the proper training?

Recap

In selecting a registration firm to perform an ISO or QS-9000 audit, a company must consider five major areas: scope, approach, accreditation, customer preference, and cost. Scope refers to the registrar's background and experience—the ability to perform a meaningful audit of a company's quality system. Approach is how a registrar conducts an audit, including its method for assessing nonconformances. Accreditation refers to where a firm's registration or "mark" is accepted; ISO registration does a company no good if no one accepts that registration as valid. A company should always ask its customers to recommend an ISO or QS-9000 registrar; some customers will accept registration only by certain auditors. Cost of registration varies from company to company and from registrar to registrar. A company should get cost estimates from all potential registrars and then assess the value of the registrar's services.

A company should inquire into the qualifications of the individual auditors. To be certified as ISO assessors, auditors must have both background in a related field and training in ISO and auditing procedures. In addition, a lead auditor must have the "people skills" necessary to direct a group of auditors and work with the company being audited.

Chapter 6

The Internal Audit

Learning Objectives

By the end of this chapter, you should be able to:

- List three reasons for staggering internal audits
- Name three of the steps in preparing for the audit
- Enumerate four things that should be included in an audit checklist
- Describe the four methods of gathering evidence

Introduction

As discussed in Chapter 4, internal audits are a crucial part of any ISO/QS program. First, both ISO and QS-9000 require that a company conduct internal audits, and the auditor who conducts the registration audit will certainly ask to see records from internal audits. Second, internal audits help a company prepare for the "real thing." By conducting regular internal audits of all aspects of its quality system, a company can assess the status of the system and how it relates to the ISO/QS-9000 standards, evaluate any improvements in the system, and correct any nonconformances before the registration audit. An internal audit also helps employees get used to the type of questions they will face from the external auditor. The third reason for internal audits is really the most important—to continuously improve your quality system.

This chapter provides a step-by-step plan for conducting a series of internal audits, from initial planning through the final report. (Note: Because the internal audit follows the same general sequence as the registration audit, this chapter is written from the perspective of the *auditor*, the person or persons doing the audit. Chapter 7, which covers the registration audit, is written from the perspective of the *auditee*, the company being audited. The procedures outlined in this chapter can also be used to audit a supplier for quality compliance.)

Internal Audits for QS-9000

While the language of QS-9000 and ISO 9000 in relation to internal audits is nearly identical, remember that QS-9000 comes with its own generic checklist for many of the requirements—the Quality System Assessment (QSA). This document should form the core for internal audits in companies seeking QS-9000. The questions that address specific procedures within a company are built around this core, as are additional questions that are required by the QS-9000 standard but not covered within the QSA instrument. Remember that the third-party registration firm will also be using a version of the QSA; employees should be prepared for the external audit by familiarizing them with these types of questions during the internal audit.

Planning Internal Audits

The first step in planning an internal audit, as with every other quality activity covered by ISO/QS-9000, is to establish a policy and procedures for conducting internal audits. The policy and procedures should do the following:

- Create a schedule for conducting audits of all quality-related functions (as defined by a company's overall quality plan)
- Ensure organizational independence and authority of the auditors, including access to top management
- Identify the persons responsible for the audit system and delineate their authority
- Establish personnel requirements, facilities, and funding to implement the audit system

The Internal Audit   **121**

- Ensure that auditors have access to facilities, personnel, and documentation required to plan and conduct the audit
- Provide a system for reporting the results of the audits to senior management and to the management of the function audited
- Create a plan for filing reports of the results of each audit and a plan for carrying out any corrective action needed to remedy nonconformances
- Establish a means of verifying that corrective action has been taken

Each of these topics is discussed in detail in this chapter.

Establishing an Audit Schedule

ISO 9001 requires "documented procedures for planning and implementing internal quality audits... Internal quality audits shall be scheduled on the basis and importance of the activity being audited..." Note that ISO does not define what the schedule should be; a company must decide this. QS-9000 is similarly vague, but the general interpretation of this clause among ISO auditors is that each function in a company that affects quality as defined by the ISO standards must be audited at least once a year. Areas/departments/functions with a large number of employees or processes, areas that have a greater effect on quality, and areas where significant nonconformances have been uncovered in the past should be audited more frequently. Other factors to be considered when determining the audit schedule include the following:

- ***Production schedule***—Some companies, especially food-processing firms, make certain products or use certain processes only at certain times during the year; audits of these processes will have to be conducted when the processes are active. Also, production managers may take a dim view of an audit being held during a particularly busy time and may be less than helpful. (The auditor should be as sensitive as possible to the needs of the audit customer. Auditors should remember that the purpose of the audit is not to find fault but to improve the system.)
- ***Maintenance schedule***—Some companies, especially steel and textile mills, cease production at certain times for major maintenance; obviously, this would not a good time for an audit of production functions—although it might be a good time to audit the maintenance department.

A company must determine the frequency of the audits for each function within the company, adhere to that schedule, and defend the schedule to the external auditor. Most companies stagger the schedule of internal audits, assessing different departments at different times. This staggering has several advantages:

1. It allows a company to stretch limited resources, especially personnel. In many companies, especially smaller firms, a handful of people will conduct all the audits. Staggering the assessments will give them time to compile their reports and still perform their other duties within the company.
2. It allows the internal auditors to "learn as they go." Most companies do not have a large pool of trained quality auditors. The people who conduct the audits typically have the technical ability for the task, but they may not be familiar with all the other skills necessary to perform an audit or with the audit procedures themselves. The internal audits are a learning process for the auditors as well as for the areas audited.
3. It minimizes disruption of the normal flow of products and services through a company.

The audit schedule should be distributed to the departments or areas to be audited so that they have plenty of time to prepare. Because ISO internal audits are audits of the system—including documentation of past performance—rather than of individual products, surprise audits accomplish little more than creating resentment of the auditor and the audit process. A nonconformance in the quality system cannot be "covered up" by a flurry of activity just before the system audit (as long as documentation is thoroughly reviewed). Table 6.1 shows a typical schedule for internal audits.

Selecting the Auditing Team

Wherever possible, audits should be conducted by a team rather than by one individual for several reasons. First, a team composed of people from various backgrounds has a diversity of skill and knowledge that cannot be found in one person. Second, the team approach ensures that the auditor will not be overwhelmed by the scope of the project and that the audit will be concluded in a timely fashion. Third, it ensures that any personal biases for or against a certain department, function, or person,

The Internal Audit

Table 6.1 Sample Schedule for ISO Internal Audits

Activity to Be Audited	Oct	Nov	Dec	Jan	Feb	Mar	Apr	May	Jun	Jul	Aug	Sep
Management responsibility					X							
Design Control		X						X				
Document Control		X										
Engineering			X					X				
Incoming Inspection				X								
Process Inspection		X					X					X
Final Inspection			X					X				
Product Line 1				X				X				
Product Line 2				X				X				
Repair Facility	X											
Personnel	X											
IMTE		X				X						
Contract Review		X								X		
Purchasing	X						X					
Warehouse					X			X				
Shipping			X				X				X	
Order Entry						X				X		
Standards Lab		X							X			

or any personal interpretations of the audit standards, will not be a factor in the conduct of the audit or in the audit report.

The team will include a team leader, or "lead auditor," and one or more persons from other areas of the company who have some expertise in the area being audited. The members of the team may vary from audit to audit, depending on the function being examined. In many cases, the lead auditor will identify a number of possible auditors throughout the company and will choose a team from among them for each audit, depending on each auditor's area of expertise.

Ideally, multisite companies will have an audit team at each location. This may not be possible for companies with a large number of small branches. In this case, the team from headquarters may have to travel to the branches to perform the audits. Companies with a number of sites in a relatively compact area may set up a regional audit team composed of members from the separate facilities to conduct assessments in any facility in that area.

The Lead Auditor

Very large companies may already have full-time quality auditors. In most companies, however, the lead auditor is generally the ISO champion or the quality manager. This person has the independence and clout a lead auditor needs, as well as some knowledge of the workings of each department to be audited. It is essential that the person designated as the internal lead auditor also be trained in proper audit procedures. It is strongly recommended that anyone who is to be a lead auditor in a mid- to large-size firm attend a five-day IRQA- or RAB-approved "lead auditor" course. In smaller companies where someone from the outside comes in to present a one- or two-day overview of ISO auditing, that individual's credentials, which should at a minimum include attendance at a IRQA/RAB-approved course and experience as an internal auditor, should be documented.

Audit Team Members

The other members of the audit team should be chosen for their technical knowledge in one or more areas, their familiarity and experience with the operation to be audited, and their ability to work as a team to conduct the audit. When selecting team members for a particular audit, the lead auditor should take care to ensure the independence of all members from the function being audited. For example, in preparing for an audit of the production department, the lead auditor should not select as a member of the team a person from production, no matter how strong his or her other qualifications may be. While this person may be able to function independently and objectively, his or her selection would not meet the ISO requirement (ISO 9001 Clause 4.17) of independence of auditors and may result in a nonconformance in the actual ISO registration audit.

Lead auditors should not be bound by traditional thinking when selecting an audit team. The leader should draw people from beyond the quality department. Engineers and technicians can contribute a great deal to an audit team, as can, in certain circumstances, production workers, especially crew leaders. Sales representatives can be valuable in assessing purchasing procedures, just as purchasing staff can be used to assess sales procedures. Secretaries who have been around the company a long time can make good auditors if given the proper training. They know much about "how things are really run" and are fluent in "management language." Experienced file clerks may know a great deal about document control procedures. The lead auditor should choose the team from as wide a base as possible, to ensure that no one perspective dominates the auditors' approach to the audit.

Think About It...

Who in your company would make good members of an internal audit team?

The number of people on the audit team should be determined by the scope of the particular audit and by the size of the department being audited. Most companies use teams of two to four people for internal audits. A larger team may take a long time to coalesce, which would have an adverse effect on the audit.

QS-9000 and the Internal Audit Process

As mentioned in the introduction to this chapter, quality system auditing is quality system auditing, whether the audit is an ISO or a QS-9000 audit. In practice however, the QS-9000 audit is different, even though the language of the internal audit requirement in both ISO and QS-9000 audit is nearly identical. Obviously, the first difference is that the QS-9000 will be more complex in that it is a far more comprehensive system of requirements.

The second factor is that QS-9000 presents the internal auditor with a blueprint called the *Quality System Assessment*. Internal auditors should use the QSA and add questions that are specific to their company's procedures. This will typically mean that the auditor's checklists will be considerably expanded beyond the QSA.

For example, under Element 4.3 (Contract Review) is Question 2: "Is there evidence of deployment of QS-9000 and customer contract requirements into the quality system?" Because you used the QSA to help you structure your QS-9000 quality system, hopefully, there are, and in your company they are included in Procedure 307. In order to assure compliance, add questions that deal with Procedure 307 into your internal audit checklist at this point.

In terms of the entire internal audit process, however, ISO and QS-9000 present only minor differences. The internal audit process as described below applies to the QS-9000 as well as to the ISO 9000 audit.

Preparing for an Audit

Once the area to be audited has been selected and the team chosen, the lead auditor must begin preparing for the audit itself. It is hardly possible to place too much emphasis on the preparation phase. Thorough preparation will ensure that the audit accomplishes both its external (meeting the requirements of ISO/QS-9000) and internal (establishing a basis for quality improvement) goals. An audit that is ill-planned almost certainly will meet neither of these goals. There are five basic steps in the preparation phase of an internal audit:

1. Determine the purpose of the audit.
2. Establish the scope for the audit.
3. Identify the performance standard to be used.
4. Review the documents and systems used in the area to be audited to gain a working knowledge of its systems, including procedures and work instructions.
5. Create a checklist to be used in the audit.

Remember that many functions within a company will share some of the same procedures and work instructions. For example, almost every function within a company shares the same document control and corrective action procedures. The auditors must audit each department's compliance with these procedures and instructions; just because one department follows them does not necessarily mean that others do. Of course, there is often a central records storage for these types of procedures; auditing these records might give auditors a hint as to which departments are not following them.

An issue that many companies face is who audits the auditors. That is, who audits the quality assurance or quality system functions? Because the auditors must be independent of the function, it can be difficult to find qualified individuals to audit the auditors. It is generally recommended that companies look for people who have audit experience and who work in a function that is not included in the quality system, such as personnel in the accounting or finance department. These people would be viewed as independent of the function being audited.

Table 6.2 Overview of One Company's Internal Audit Process*

Notification
1. Determine the date of the audit by checking your calendar and contacting the manager and agreeing on the date. This should be done a minimum of two weeks and preferably three weeks prior to the audit. *Allow two to four hours for most department audits and at least one full day and preferably one-and-a-half days to audit an individual office!*
2. Complete the "Audit Notification" form.
3. Send the original "Notification" to the manager of the area/office being audited.
4. Send the copy of the "Notification" to Jane MacDonald (Quality Manager).
5. Confirm the date and time of the opening meeting with the department manager two to five days prior to the audit.

Personal and Team Preparation
1. Obtain uncontrolled copies of the procedures to be audited and previous internal audits from Joan Johnson (Files Maintenance Secretary).
2. Obtain uncontrolled copies of "Master Lists of Forms" and "Quality Records" from Joan Johnson. Also obtain updated "Table of Revisions."
3. Review the procedures/master lists with your team members; make note of:
   a. Changes to the procedure since the last audit
   b. Documentation requirements/quality records
   c. Forms
4. Create checklists for the audit:
   a. Questions for those to be interviewed—include generic questions.
   b. Documentation to be examined to prove procedure is being followed—this includes quality records, forms, and other relevant documents.
   (*Note:* You may refer to previous checklists, but remember that the procedure may have changed, and you don't want to ask a question that no longer applies.)
5. Determine who you would like to interview.
   (*Note:* This step applies in particular to departments with more than three people, such as Inside Sales.)
   a. Review the previous audit to see who was interviewed during that audit.
   b. Review the department personnel list to see whom you should talk to.
   c. Determine which auditor will lead the interview with which individual.
   At the end of all of this, you should know:
   - Whom you will talk to
   - What you will ask (including generic questions)
   - What documentation you will look at

Conducting the Audit
1. Arrive on time for the opening meeting; ask that a conference room or office be made available to you during the audit.
2. Be firm but flexible—ask for the people on your list.
3. Spend time with the people to be interviewed; if they waffle, probe. *(Be prepared to expand the scope of the audit if you find lack of knowledge or implementation of a procedure. Is it just one individual or is it systemic?)*

Table 6.2 Overview of One Company's Internal Audit Process* (continued)

4. Check the procedures manuals for currency and conformity. Check the "Table of Revisions."
5. After two or three audit interviews, retire to the conference room to discuss the progress of the audit with your auditor. Change of direction? This may also be a good place to review some of the documentation.
6. After interviews and review of records and forms, conduct a closing meeting with the department manager. Outline your findings, but do not go into minute detail or get into long discussions/debates about whether something is a nonconformance or not—nobody wants a nonconformance.
7. At the end of the audit, document nonconformances on the approved form. Hold closing meeting with the auditee. Write the report using Form B and submit to quality manager within 14 days of finishing the audit.

* This document is not the company's procedure; it is a handout that is part of its internal auditor training.

Note: Even though the internal audit schedule is distributed throughout a company, as part of the preparation stage, the lead auditor should notify the head of the function to be audited in writing at least two weeks before the audit is scheduled. This is a courtesy as well as insurance against the schedule being lost or overlooked. Table 6.2 provides a general overview of how the internal audit process operates in one mid-sized company.

The Purpose of the Audit

The purpose of the internal audit would appear to be simple enough: to see how a particular area of a company complies with the internal procedures and ISO/QS-9000 requirements for that function. However, the audit can and should go beyond that. The audit can also identify areas for quality improvement in the function being audited. Rather than just noting nonconformances in a particular area, the internal auditors should help the manager and staff of that department identify the causes of the nonconformance so that they can be eliminated. The internal auditors should try to find nonconformances and eliminate them before the ISO auditor arrives. It is not uncommon during an internal audit for an auditor to find a borderline nonconformance—something that is almost but not quite a nonconformance. Frequently, the auditor also will find that an employee understands a process better after the auditor has asked him or her about it and had the employee explain the procedure.

The Scope of the Audit

The scope of the audit is the area to be covered. In an internal audit of a certain department, scope comes down to one question: Will the entire function be audited or will the audit be limited? The answer to that question depends upon the function itself. An audit of sales, for example, may cover only contract review and sales' input to design control, the two sales-related elements covered by ISO 9001. In purchasing, the audit may be limited only to procedures involved in purchasing raw materials and subassemblies for the company's process (areas addressed by the ISO 9000 requirements) and not to procedures involved in purchasing materials for internal use, like office supplies.

An audit of production, conversely, generally will be an audit of the entire function, from the inspection of incoming materials to the storage, packaging, and delivery of the finished product. Design departments often will receive a functional review that begins with planning and ranges through the design output, verification, and design change process. Records, of course, will receive particular attention.

Identify the Performance Standards

Identifying performance standards is more complex than it appears on the surface. The general standard is, of course, the standard to which a company is seeking to become registered (ISO 9001, 9002 , 9003, or QS-9000). However, the requirements of the ISO standards are couched in general terms; it is up to each company to establish its own specific standards within the ISO framework. These specific standards are contained in a company's policies, procedures, and work instructions. It is these policies, procedures, and work instructions that are the actual standards against which a function's performance must be measured. (The ISO auditor will examine the policies, procedures, and work instruction to ensure that they meet the intent of the standards.)

For example, ISO 9001 Clause 4.11.2, Inspection, Measuring and Test Equipment, Subclause (b) says that the supplier shall "identify all inspection, measuring and test equipment that can affect product quality and calibrate and adjust them at prescribed intervals…" Obviously, an auditor cannot determine if a company is in compliance with this requirement because there is no way to determine exactly what the indefinite term *prescribed* means. An auditor can determine, however, if a department is in compliance with company policy 4.11.2 (b), which says, "All inspection measuring and test equipment and devices that can affect product quality shall be calibrated and adjusted on a weekly (daily, monthly, etc.) basis."

Review the Systems to Be Audited

The audit team should review the documents pertaining to the function to be audited before beginning the audit. These documents include policies, procedures, work instructions, a list of equipment, engineering documents, and results of past audits, including corrective action recommended and taken. (It is especially important that the auditor make certain that any nonconformances noted in previous audits have been corrected and that the corrective actions have been maintained.) This review has three benefits:

1. It allows the audit team members to become familiar with the formal control systems of the department.
2. It allows them to plan the audit.
3. It suggests areas to examine for possible nonconformance.

The lead auditor should retrieve the documents from the company's document control area at least two weeks in advance. Each team member should review the documents related to his or her specialty (production control, inspection and testing, etc.) and prepare a list of questions to help in conducting the audit.

Think About It...

If you were conducting an audit of your department, what documents would you examine before beginning?

Creating the Checklist for the Audit

A checklist is essential to every audit. A good checklist provides a logical road map or guide for conducting the audit; ensures that all aspects of the audit are covered; saves time during the audit because questions are prepared in advance; allows for a wide range of responses to audit questions; accommodates interview, observation, and sampling results; and provides a guideline for creating the final audit report. Another advantage of the checklist is that it helps minimize variation and subjectivity in the audit process. Every audit has some subjectivity inherent in the process. While the auditor relies on objective evidence, the auditor's personal experience, strengths, and skills will always be a part of any audit process. Having a checklist with specified criteria ensures objectivity despite different skill and knowledge levels among the auditors conducting the audit. As noted above, many registrars today will examine the checklists for evidence of conducting a thorough internal audit.

Organizing the Checklist

The overall audit checklist is composed of smaller checklists covering each area of the function to be audited. The lead auditor is responsible for selecting or creating a form for the checklists and providing copies of these forms to the individual auditors. Each auditor will enter any questions about the area to which he or she has been assigned. The lead auditor checks the questions to ensure that the auditor is being objective and to ensure that no important areas are omitted. As each auditor conducts his or her portion of the audit, he or she will write the answers to each question (obtained through interviews, observations, or sampling) on the appropriate page. When the audit is concluded, the lead auditor will assemble the individual pages into a final checklist which will be used to prepare the final report.

The best way for each auditor to assemble his or her checklist questions is to break down each requirement into manageable segments and then set up a series of "yes or no" questions. For example, in judging compliance with Procedure 4.11, "All inspection measuring and test equipment and devices that can affect product quality shall be calibrated and adjusted once each month," the auditor might restate the requirement as a question: "Has the following equipment been calibrated in the last month?" The auditor would then list each piece of equipment, leaving space for a "yes" or a "no" after each item. He or she would also leave a space for information on how the answer was obtained (for example, "Tag shows equipment calibrated on July 6, 1996; this is within allowed parameters").

In smaller companies with fewer than 50 procedures, it is a good idea to set up a two-day internal auditor training program. One of the days can be devoted to writing checklists for the procedures, so that the internal auditors can begin the audit process with most if not all checklists completed.

Contents of a Checklist

One page from a generic checklist is shown in Figure 6.1. A checklist showing the internal auditor's comments is provided in Figure 6.2. Other types of checklists are available as well. The form used in conducting an audit is strictly a matter of personal preference (check whether the auditor/registrar has a preference), as long as it contains the following elements:

- Document control information (a reference number, date, page number)
- Information on the auditor and auditee (name of the auditor, name of company and department being audited, name of the contact in that department)
- The standard to which the audit is conducted and the requirement(s) for the particular operation covered on each page
- The question(s) asked and the method(s) used to verify the answers
- A space to include findings, particularly nonconformances
- A space to indicate status of the process (Does it meet the requirements? If not, why not?)
- A space to list further action (corrective action, additional monitoring)
- A space to verify that corrective action was carried out and was effective

In most cases, these checklist forms can be used for subsequent audits of the same functions. With different questions, the forms can also be used for other internal audits (or audits of suppliers). This ability to reuse checklist forms keeps the lead auditor from having to reinvent the wheel for each audit. However, it is important to remember to update the checklist to meet the requirements of a revised procedure.

Many consulting firms offer standardized checklists that are touted to be effective in any audit situation. While these checklists can help an auditor assure that a company's quality system generally meets the intent

The Internal Audit 133

		YES	NO

4 Quality System Requirements

4.1 Management Responsibility

4.1.1 Quality Policy
1. Does the company have a written mission statement on quality? ____ ____
2. Has the company management clearly defined and documented quality policy and objectives? ____ ____
3. Has company management demonstrated its commitment to quality? If so, how? ____ ____
4. Has the company policy on quality been explained to all associates within the company? ____ ____
5. Is the quality policy implemented and systematically maintained throughout the organization? ____ ____

Notes: _____
_____
_____
_____

4.1.2 Organization

4.1.2.1 Responsibility and Authority
1. Have the authority and responsibility, as well as the interrelationships of all associates who manage, perform, and verify work, been clearly defined? ____ ____
2. Is there a person or group within the organization that has the freedom and authority to initiate action to prevent occurrence of product nonconformity? ____ ____
3. Is there a person or group with the responsibility to identify and record any product quality problems? ____ ____
4. Is there a person or group with the freedom and authority to initiate, recommend, or provide solutions through designated channels? ____ ____
5. Is there a defined way to verify the implementation of these solutions? ____ ____
6. Is there a person or group with the freedom and authority to control further processing, delivery, or installation of nonconforming product or services until the deficiency or unsatisfactory condition has been corrected? ____ ____

Notes: _____
_____
_____
_____

Figure 6.1 ISO 9000 Checklist for Internal Quality Audits

GKI	Internal Quality Audit	Page 1 of 1 Date: 1-14-96 No. 10 Rev. 0

Audit Subject: Inspection and Testing	Organization Audited: QC Lab
Audited by: Donald M. Wall	Contacted: Jim Henry, QC Lab Supervisor
Requirements: (Requirement to be stated from reference) All lab technicians will follow written procedures for in-process inspection and testing.	Req. Ref.: Q-91 4.9 Quality Manual Sec. 9 Procedure 9-72a

Question and Verification Method: Interview J. Kelly, B. Farmer, lab technicians, J. Henry, lab supervisor; review procedure manuals.

Findings/NCRs: The lab has written procedures for all test methods. However, the only current revisions of the procedures and JWIs are found in the lab in the lab supervisor's office. The lab technicians work from outdated procedures unless they check with the lab supervisor. (NCR 960101)

Follow-up Action:			
Who: QA Manager	What: Needs to meet with Jim Henry to determine how many current manuals should be in the lab (document control)	By When: Feb. 5, 1996	Remarks: Affects document control (4.5) and inspection and testing (4.9)

Figure 6.2   Sample Internal Audit Checklist

of the standard, they are frequently not that effective by themselves because they cannot reflect how a particular company operates—particular features of its control system, its pattern for assigning responsibility, and the quirks that make it unique. Nonetheless, a standardized list can be helpful to the beginning auditor because it provides a starting point—

a set of established questions to draw upon and adapt to fit a company's system. As the system matures and the auditor gains experience, the checklist can be improved and made more consistent with the company's own quality system.

The QSA is actually one such generic checklist. But it is only effective when questions from a company's procedures are integrated into the checklist.

The Initial Meeting

Like the ISO/QS registration audit, the internal audit begins with a meeting between the audit team and representatives (generally the department head and a few supervisors or lead workers) of the function to be audited. The lead auditor starts the meeting by introducing the members of the audit team (even if it is only the lead auditor and one other person). He or she should allow each member of the audit team a few moments to describe their qualifications and explain what areas they will be auditing. The lead auditor discusses the scope of the audit, detailing which areas of the function will be covered by the audit and which, if any, will not.

The lead auditor also explains the methods that will be used to determine compliance with the requirements. He or she provides the auditee with a list of the information that will be sampled and gets approval from the department head for the auditors to interview workers. The lead auditor shows the auditee the checklists that will be used in the audit and explains briefly what the auditors will do if a nonconformance is found.

Most important, the lead auditor will take time to explain the purpose of the audit, emphasizing that it is not to find fault with people but to detect problems with the system. The lead auditor should help the people in the department being audited to understand that it is far better for the internal audit team to find areas that need corrective action than for the ISO auditor to find those problems. Understanding this will help them get over any fears they may have about being audited.

Set the Audit Schedule

The next step is to discuss the schedule for the audit. The lead auditor should have a schedule prepared, detailing which areas will be examined when, but should be prepared to change it if necessary, depending on contingencies discovered during the initial meeting. If, for example, the production line, which was to be examined first, has been stopped for emergency maintenance, the lead auditor should reschedule that particular operation later in the audit.

The lead auditor also should discuss other matters of logistics, such as a place for the audit team members to meet, luncheon facilities and plans, and whether the auditors will need special passes, escorts, or safety equipment to visit certain areas. In small, one-site companies, these matters may not be a concern. However, if some or all of the auditors are from another site, these matters need to be addressed.

Establish a Positive Tone

The initial meeting will set the tone for the entire audit. It is essential that the audit team establish a positive tone during this meeting and continue it throughout the audit. The members of the audit team, especially the lead auditor, must be friendly but businesslike. The representatives of the function to be audited may be apprehensive or resentful of this intrusion into their work space and the possible consequences, especially if this is the first time the department has been audited. The auditors must go out of their way to ease this apprehension or resentment. They can do this by emphasizing the positive nature of the audit (the opportunity for quality improvement) rather than the negative (the search for nonconformances). While the phrase "I'm from the head office and I'm here to help" is generally treated as a joke, the auditors can make it a reality by working with, not against, members of the department they are auditing to achieve the common goal.

The lead auditor should ask the department head if there is any area of which he or she is particularly proud. Some departments in a company, and some individuals within a department, look forward to an audit and are proud of what they have accomplished and how their functions operate, and they welcome outside corroboration. Giving them an opportunity to shine will make them more cooperative in other areas of the audit, give a positive cast to the audit, and make the audit easier and more pleasant for the audit team.

The audit team also can help establish rapport and create a positive tone for the audit by including a question-and-answer period in the initial meeting. The auditee usually will have a number of questions about the audit process (especially if it is a first-time audit), and the lead auditor should answer all questions as fully as possible.

On the other hand, the auditors must take care not to be too friendly. They must present a businesslike demeanor to overcome any attitude on the part of the audited function that this is not a real audit. This attitude is especially likely in a small company, where some or all of the auditee representatives may know some or all of the auditors. It is essential that the audit team present an air of professionalism to show that this assessment is, indeed, real and that nonconformances will be taken seriously, will be reported, and must be addressed by the auditee. Remember, the goals of the internal audit are to improve the system and to detect nonconformances before the registrar does.

Performing the Audit

The first step in performing the audit is to understand the control systems used in the department. In most cases, there will be two systems—formal and informal. The formal system is what is described in the documentation the auditor examined during the preparation phase. The formal system describes things as they should be. The informal system, on the other hand, is how things are. In almost every case, there will be some deviation between the two systems. One part of the auditor's job is to compare the actual process with the idealized version. This process is called verifying the system. It involves gathering evidence to prove (1) that the system works exactly as described in the documentation or (2) that it does not. Four methods are used by the auditor to gather evidence during the audit: observing, sampling, tracing, and interviewing.

Observing

Yogi Berra once said, "You can observe a lot by just watching." While simplistic, this statement contains a lot of truth for the auditor. A good auditor is constantly alert on his or her tour through the function being audited. As important as other methods of gathering evidence are, there is no substitute for attentive observation—which in this case means using all the senses. For example, an auditor should not hesitate to ask such questions as: "Why does it smell like something is burning?" "Is that machine always that noisy" "Should the machine feel that hot at this distance?" The most obvious potential nonconformance is often overlooked. For example, one company that sold industrial chain had no consistent method to measure or cut random lengths of chain.

A few moments of scrutiny are often enough to determine if a particular process is in compliance with the standards. For example, the auditor frequently can tell with a glance if nonconforming material is properly labeled and segregated, if proper storage and handling techniques are used, or if employees are following the prescribed procedures or work instructions. At the very least, observing will suggest questions that need to be explored further through sampling or interviewing.

Sampling

Sampling is one of the most effective methods of acquiring evidence in an audit. Sampling is the process of examining a number of examples of a product or documents to project a picture of the whole. In most cases, it is physically impossible, or at least impractical, to examine every product or every document; auditors can use sampling as a way to gather evidence in a relatively short period of time. There are four advantages to sampling: (1) the sample size can be determined in advance; (2) the result can be compared to 100 percent examination; (3) it conserves time; and (4) the result is unbiased, defensible, and objective and can be reasonably duplicated by anyone.

If sampling is to produce a true picture of the process as a whole, the auditor must answer four questions before beginning:

1. What is to be sampled?
2. What will the results mean?
3. How large should the sample be?
4. How is the sample to be gathered?

What Is to Be Sampled?

Even though sampling is a great time and labor saver, outside constraints often limit the amount of sampling that can be done. Therefore, the auditor should sample only crucial items. The auditor can determine many of the areas where sampling will be especially effective from examination of documentation (done in the preparation phase) or from information gained in interviews with workers in the department. Areas to examine include points where two processes meet or where responsibility for a process passes from one organization to another, new processes which involve a learning curve, processes that are overloaded or where there are not enough people to ensure proper controls, and processes that have a history of inefficiencies or defects.

What Will the Results Mean?

Obviously, sampling will not be 100 percent accurate. The auditor's goal should be 90 to 95 percent accuracy. This percentage of accuracy is known as the *confidence factor*. It is generally expressed as a probability of a percentage of defects or nonconformities (e.g., "I am 95 percent confident that no more than 3 percent of products are nonconforming" or "I am 95 percent confident that the compliance factor is at least 97 percent").

How Large Should the Sample Be?

The size of the sample to be taken is determined by the size of the whole, the confidence factor which the auditor wishes to achieve, and the percentage of defects that exist. Obviously, the larger the population (the total number of items) and the higher the desired confidence factor, the larger the sample must be. Choosing a sample that is too small may lead to an erroneous conclusion. For example, suppose an auditor is to check 1,000 contracts for evidence of the review required by ISO 9001. She chooses three contracts, none of which bear signatures indicating review. This could mean that no contracts were reviewed. It also could mean that of 1,000 contracts, only 3 (three-tenths of 1 percent) were not signed, and she just happened to pick those three. The answer most likely is somewhere in the middle of these extremes, but exactly where cannot be determined with so small a sample. The sample must be large enough to eliminate any mathematical oddities and ensure the desired confidence factor. However, an extremely large sample may be very costly in terms of time and other resources.

In reporting the results of sampling, the auditor must be careful not to nitpick. If, for example, in examining contracts for signs of review, the auditor finds evidence that all reviews were conducted but finds a few incorrect page numbers, such a finding probably is not worth mentioning in the report. (However, it may be a sign of a larger document control problem, and the auditor should keep it in mind.) Putting that sort of detail in a report is liable to evoke a "so what" response from the auditee, and a large number of "so whats" may cause the auditee to not take the audit seriously.

The auditor also should avoid exhausting detail and include only main findings in the report. For example, if an auditor samples 50 contracts and finds that 18 show no signs of having been reviewed, he or she should say in the report, "In a sample of 50 contracts, 18 bore no signatures indicating review" or "In a sample of 50 contracts, fully one-third bore no signatures indicating review." The auditor should not get into a long discussion of statistical probabilities; the simple statement is enough to get the auditee's attention.

How Is the Sample to Be Gathered?

All samples should be chosen at random. The auditor should not take the first 50 products he or she finds but should take samples at random until reaching the required sample size. Random selection should ensure that the samples are representative of the whole and that any nonconformities found reflect on the whole process, not just one part of it.

Whatever the method used for sampling, the auditor must personally do the selecting. The auditor should not accept samples offered by the auditee or allow the auditee to "steer" him or her to certain samples. After all, what would you select if an auditor asked you for a sample? Surely, only those conforming to requirements.

Note: Sampling—if done properly—is a complicated process. The details are too numerous to cover here. Those planning to include sampling as part of internal audits should consult one of the numerous reference texts available.

Think About It...

If you were conducting an audit of your department, what processes would you want to sample? How would you go about sampling them?

Tracing

Tracing involves following the steps of a process from beginning to end (or, in some cases, backwards to the beginning from the end). Tracing helps the auditor "get inside" the process to understand it better. It also may uncover some discrepancies that are not apparent from the outside.

To trace a process, the auditor selects the procedure or work instruction to trace. The auditor gets the documentation on the procedure or work instruction to establish its supposed path and then follows a particular item, such as a product, a purchase order, or a shipping request, through that path to see if that is, indeed, how it progresses. A process flow diagram (PFD) is a good tool to use when tracing. If the function being audited does not have PFDs to accompany its procedures, the auditor may want to make a rough sketch in order to understand the process better.

Interviewing

Interviewing is probably the most crucial skill in the auditor's repertoire. Unfortunately, it is a skill which many auditors lack. An auditor can become so obsessed with numbers that he or she forgets the human element. The lead auditor, at least, should be thoroughly trained in communication techniques, and it is a good idea for the other auditors to be trained as well.

The auditor will not interview everyone in a particular job function. The auditor should choose people who are in a position to provide objective evidence or who can clear up questions the auditor may have about any aspect of the process. For example, if the auditor wants to determine if a particular procedure or work instruction is regularly followed, he or she should ask two or three people who do that task to describe the steps they follow in performing their jobs. Interviewing involves four basic steps:

1. Put the subject (the person being interviewed) at ease.
2. Explain the purpose of the interview.
3. Ask questions that are likely to evoke solid answers.
4. Listen to what the person has to say.

(*Note:* The information presented here on interviewing is written on the basis of a one-on-one interview. With minor adjustments, it can be applied to group interviews as well.)

Put the Subject at Ease

A person being interviewed by an auditor is likely to be somewhat nervous. The person may be confused about exactly what the audit means to the department and to him or her or may be concerned about reprisals if he or she "spills the beans." The auditor should present a friendly but businesslike demeanor and should take steps to overcome the subject's initial nervousness. Depending on the person involved, this could involve anything from a simple introduction and handshake to a brief discussion about the weather or some other topic of interest. The auditor should not proceed with the interview until he or she feels that any barriers to effective communication have been removed. However, the auditor should also take care to avoid getting bogged down in trivial small talk.

Explain the Purpose of the Interview

In most cases, every employee in the department will know who the auditor is and what the auditor is doing there within ten minutes after he or she sets foot in the door. Nonetheless, it is important for the auditor to explain the exact purpose of the interview, for two reasons. First, it helps overcome any unease the employee may feel. Second, it makes the interview personal—and the auditor wants the employee's help in gathering information. In most cases, this explanation will make the employee feel more at ease and will help the employee "open up" to the auditor.

In the early stages of the interview, the auditor must demonstrate his or her competence. The best way for an auditor to do this is to be well organized and to demonstrate an understanding of the subject being discussed. However, the auditor should avoid saying too much about the subject. At best, the auditor may be perceived as a showoff; at worst, the auditor she may give away answers to questions on the checklist. The auditor should remember that the purpose of the interview is to learn, not to teach. Good auditors are good listeners.

Ask Questions and Listen to the Answers

The auditor should use the questions on his or her checklist as the basis for the interview. The interview should start off with open-ended questions (i.e., questions that require more than a yes or no answer). Examples include:

- When you first start to put the assembly together, what is the first step?
- After you take the customer's information, what do you do with the order form?

- Where does the assembly go after you have attached the framistan?
- What is the procedure if an approved vendor is not available?
- How do you assure that customer complaints are logged and are acted upon?
- How do you separate returned goods from goods that are about to be shipped to the customer?

The auditor should remember that asking a question is only the first part of the process. A good internal auditor will listen very carefully to the answer to make sure that there is real content, not just fluff, in the answer and that the answer is complete. If the employee's answer is not complete or is unclear, the auditor should follow up by asking: "What is the next step?" or "Can you give me an example of a time when this occurred?" or "Can you show me exactly how you do this?" The auditor may have to prod the employee several times to get a complete answer. At the end of the employee's answer, the auditor may need to ask a direct, or closed, question, such as: "At that point, are you finished with your part of the operation?"

The auditor should remember to take notes; taking notes shows that the information is important and that the interview is serious. This is especially important in small companies where the auditor may know the person being interviewed personally. It is also a good idea for the auditor to "write out loud," that is, read the notes as he or she writes them and ask the employee if that is indeed what he or she really means.

The auditor should avoid asking leading questions. These questions suppose that the auditor already knows the answer and is seeking corroboration or is trying to "catch" the employee. An example of this type of question is: "I understand that when you're done you write the time down on a product completion list. Is this correct?" The main problem with this type of question is that the auditor will get the answer that the employee thinks the auditor wants—and that may not always be the truth.

Hundreds of books have been written on nonverbal communication or body language, the gestures and postures that people use when they talk which often communicate more information more truthfully than the actual words. Body language is entirely too complicated a subject to be discussed in this book. Suffice it to say that the auditor should read at least one of these books so he or she can interpret what the employee "says" silently.

One mistake new auditors frequently make is being so anxious to complete their checklists that they overlook the opportunity to probe when an answer is incorrect or incomplete or when it conflicts with a previous answer. Auditors should listen to the answer to each question and be prepared to backtrack and ask the question in a different way or take a new direction if necessary.

After the Interview

When the interview is completed, the auditor should share any tentative conclusions with the employee. If the auditor's initial analysis indicates that the system is working as it should, the auditor should let the employee know that he or she is doing the right thing. If, on the other hand, there seems to be a discrepancy, or if the employee has given an answer that seems to contradict information gathered from sampling, observation, or previous interviews, the auditor should make an effort to reconcile the two versions. The auditor should not assume that the employee is lying or does not understand the process. The employee may have inadvertently left out information or may be flustered or nervous. It is also possible that the auditor misunderstood the explanation. Whatever the reason, the auditor should question the employee until the matter is resolved.

The auditor should then tell the employee what the next step is. If the auditor has gotten all the information needed from the employee, the auditor should tell the employee so, emphasizing that the employee has done a good job (which is most important from the employee's point of view) and that the interview is finished. If, however, the auditor thinks the employee has more information that may be helpful but cannot continue the interview because some facts need to be checked before asking any more questions, the auditor should make another appointment. The auditor should not worry about the extra time involved.

Think About It...

How would you go about interviewing someone in your department to find out how the person performs his or her job?

It is a good idea to retire to a work area after every three or four interviews to review notes, gather thoughts, and assure that any aspect of the control system that has been overlooked is examined at the next interview.

Corroboration and Conclusions

In all evidence gathering, the auditor should look for evidence that corroborates (confirms or backs up) the effective implementation of the documented system or evidence that corroborates the conclusion that the system is not working properly. Frequently, one auditor will find some evidence of a nonconformance in one area of a department, while another auditor will find corroborating evidence in another area. When they compare notes, they discover that a nonconformance exists. This can also happen in different audits, such as an audit in shipping uncovering evidence of a nonconformity in sales. For example, a sales order for a particular customer shows that the customer ordered 1,000 widgets. However, the shipping log shows that 1,040 were shipped. There is no paperwork to show that the order was changed. This is evidence of a nonconformity.

Auditors also must beware of the halo effect. As discussed earlier, this comes into play when the initial experience the auditor has with the function being audited is a positive one. When all the answers are correct and all the data are available for the first day of the audit, the auditor begins to assume that the company is totally prepared and can do no wrong. The auditor tends to get "lulled to sleep" and may not search for evidence of nonconformance, instead just accepting what he or she is given. For example, an auditor asks if all welders of a critical process have valid certificates, and the department representative says, "Yes, of course they do." If the auditor is under the spell of the halo effect, he or she will accept that answer without going to the files to examine the certificates, dates, and correspondence of the welders. Consequently, a nonconformance could pass undetected. The more things that go right during an audit, the more likely the halo effect is to come into play. An auditor has to be vigilant throughout the entire audit. Obviously, this is also a lesson for a company or department being audited.

Team Meeting

If the audit lasts more than one day (which is unusual during a single-department or -function internal audit), the audit team should meet at the end of each day to share facts, tentative conclusions, and findings (evidence of problems) uncovered during the day. This sharing may bring corroborating evidence of a problem to light. Is there an area that has done extremely well or extremely poorly? Do the facts gathered by each individual auditor point to a general conclusion? Does the audit seem to be achieving its objective?

At this time, the audit team should plan the next day's activities. The schedule may have to be changed if areas covered during the first day need further exploration. Are additional interviews or sampling necessary? Do the checklists need to be expanded?

The audit team also should have a brief meeting at the completion of the audit (if it ends during the middle of the day). It is during these meetings that the lead auditor starts preparing the audit report (see below).

After the team meeting, the lead auditor should meet with a representative from the function being audited to inform him or her of the information discussed in the audit team meeting. The lead auditor should advise the auditee of any tentative conclusions the team has reached and any changes to the schedule. (If time is a problem, or if part of the audit is conducted during second or third shift, the lead auditor can meet with the auditee representative first thing the next morning.)

The Final Meeting

Once the auditing phase is completed, the reporting phase begins. The first step is to hold a final meeting with the auditee. This meeting involves the full audit team and the same representatives of the department who attended the initial meeting. Sometimes, company executives may also attend this meeting. During an internal audit, this meeting may have to be postponed for a couple of days to assure that the people who need to attend the meeting (e.g., department managers) are able to do so.

The lead auditor prepares the team's report for this meeting, using the data gathered by the auditors and discussed during the audit team meetings. Because of time constraints, the report will be in rough form, but it should contain all the findings (evidence of nonconformance) and observations from the audit. Nothing should be held back for the formal written report. However, the auditor does not need to be too detailed in this oral report. He or she should concentrate on general findings and conclusions. For example, it is enough to say, "The audit team found 10 separate instances out of 50 samples where contracts bore no signs of review. This indicates a serious problem with the contract review process." The lead auditor does not have to mention the actual contracts that were in noncompliance. (However, if the auditee asks which contracts were involved, the lead auditor should supply that information.)

It is essential that the audit team present a "united front" during this meeting. It is not uncommon for the audit team members to disagree on some of the conclusions based on evidence uncovered during the audit. One member may think the evidence is a sign of a major nonconformance, while a second thinks more evidence is needed and a third holds that the nonconformance is there but is less serious. However, these disagreements must be resolved during the audit team's private meetings, and team members much reach consensus before reporting to the auditee. This is where the lead auditor's people skills and reliance on objective evidence can make a difficult situation acceptable to everyone. Disagreement in front of the auditee will have a major negative effect on the auditee's acceptance of the report ("If you auditors don't agree, why should we accept the results of your findings?").

Final Meeting Procedures

The lead auditor chairs the meeting. He or she should start by thanking the auditees for their cooperation during the audit and then proceed with an overall review of the audit, including areas covered and the methods used for gathering evidence. The lead auditor then should talk about the positive things the audit team has found (the things that were in compliance with the requirements). This positive beginning helps reduce any negative feelings or resentment that inevitably arise when talking about nonconformances.

When the lead auditor discusses the nonconformances, he or she should speak in a matter-of-fact, completely businesslike tone of voice. Talking down to the department representatives or using a condemnatory tone may cause the auditees to become hostile or react negatively to the audit. The lead auditor should point out each nonconformance, cite the general evidence that led to that finding, and give any recommendations for corrective action. (Recommendations should be given only during an internal audit. They should not be given during an audit of a supplier or during a third-party audit. Recommendations from an auditor invariably will be taken as "You must do it this way," or "If you do it this way, I guarantee you'll pass the audit," which may not be the case. In the same vein, the ISO/QS-9000 registration auditor will not make any specific recommendations for specific corrective actions. In both cases, the auditee must determine his or her own course of corrective action, based on the auditor's findings. This is not as crucial in the case of an internal audit because the auditor and the auditee are "on the same side.")

The lead auditor should expect some argument from the auditee. After all, the lead auditor has just presented information that may make the department look bad. The auditor should try to consider the auditee's viewpoint. When one of the auditees objects to one of the findings presented in the report, the lead auditor should not react negatively. Instead, he or she should listen carefully to the objection and then counter it with objective evidence or some other finding. For example, if the company policy states that the department head will review all contracts valued between $100,000 and $200,000 and the auditee says that contracts were not reviewed during the week she was on vacation, the auditor should point out that this was a serious nonconformance found in a review of 50 contracts and that this demonstrates a serious failure within the quality system.

The lead auditor should keep the final meeting as brief as possible but still cover all areas of the report and listen to any relevant evidence the auditees wish to present to counter the findings. However, the lead auditor should be careful not to let the meeting break down into an "us versus them" gripe session and also should not let the auditees get into a discussion regarding possible solutions. This distracts the participants from the purpose of the oral audit report and likely will dilute the effect of the report. If it becomes necessary, the auditor should say, "This is just a report, not a fault-finding or solution-finding session. You may brainstorm solutions after the report, but please allow me to continue. The purpose of this meeting is to report findings, not solve problems."

Once all relevant findings and observations have been made and the auditees have had a chance to present their case, the lead auditor should end the meeting. The meeting should conclude with both sides having reached agreement on the findings of the audit and the areas in which corrective actions are needed.

The Final Report

Within two weeks of the end of the audit (less time if possible or if required by the audit procedure), the audit team should issue a final written report on the results of the audit. This written report should contain the same information presented in the oral report; there should be no surprises unless something important was overlooked in the oral report. If this happens, the auditor should include an explanation of why the important finding was overlooked. There should be no delay in issuing the final report because each day it is delayed will decrease the importance the auditee gives it. The auditee probably will delay any corrective action until the final report is received.

The report should begin with a summary of exactly how the function is operating. It should cover the entire scope of the audit because it may be the only part company executives will read. The summary should include both areas that are functioning well, as well as areas in which nonconformances were noted and improvement is needed. The findings (nonconformances) should be summarized.

The body of the report should detail the nonconformances and the evidence that supports them. The nonconformances should be as generic as possible. As an example, consider the following findings:

- Out-of-date work instructions were being used at four separate locations throughout the department.
- Three workstations had no access to work instructions.
- Three process flow diagrams were corrected in red ink, each in a different handwriting, with no signature denoting the person initiating the change.
- Inspection reports were missing information for certain dates, as required by Procedure 4.9.4.

These pieces of evidence should be consolidated into one generic nonconformance: "Work instruction documents are not properly controlled." The report should emphasize that corrective action is needed to remedy each of the nonconformances included in the report.

In many cases, the reaction to a finding similar to the one above will be either a yawn or "so what." In the final report, the lead auditor should take pains to make the finding relevant to the auditee and impress upon the auditee how the nonconformance affects quality at the company. The auditor must answer the auditee's unspoken question—"What's in it for me?—in order for the report to be taken seriously.

Corrective Action

Upon receiving the report, the auditee must respond within a given period, usually 14 days for an internal audit or 30 for an external audit. This response will detail the corrective action the auditee has taken or intends to take to remedy the nonconformances mentioned in the audit report. In almost every case, some corrective action will be necessary.

(If no nonconformances are found, which does occasionally happen, either the auditors didn't do their jobs properly or the department is exceptional.

The auditor is responsible for assessing the corrective actions taken or planned by the auditee and ensuring that they are sufficient to remedy the nonconformances. In the case of minor nonconformances, the auditor generally will accept written notice from the auditee that the corrective actions have been taken and the nonconformances have been remedied. In the case of more serious nonconformances, the auditor should schedule a re-audit of the particular areas in which the nonconformances were noted.

Recap

Internal audits are an essential part of a company's ISO compliance program, both because they are required by ISO/QS-9000 and because they help a company uncover and remedy nonconformances before the registration audit. The steps involved in an internal audit include selecting an audit team, setting a schedule, studying documentation, preparing a checklist, holding an initial meeting, gathering evidence (through observation, sampling, tracing, and interviewing), holding a final meeting, issuing a report, initiating corrective action (on the part of the auditee), and assessing that corrective action to ensure (on the part of the auditor) that it is effective. The keys to a successful internal audit are preparation, diligence, and the "people skills" of the auditor.

Chapter 7

The Registration Audit

Learning Objectives

By the end of this chapter, you should be able to:

- List three things accomplished at the pre-audit meeting
- Explain the difference between a major nonconformance and a minor nonconformance
- List the typical components of a nonconformance report
- Describe how to initiate corrective action to remedy a nonconformance

Introduction

The ISO or QS-9000 registration audit is, in many ways, the culmination of the process, the event that brings all the preparations together and makes all the work worthwhile; successful completion of the audit means a company receives ISO or QS-9000 registration. A company becomes registered if all its people are prepared, if the company's quality system is functioning as it should be, and if the company knows how to present its case to the auditor in a way that makes it easy for him or her to understand.

Chapter 6 discussed the internal audit, the last step before the pre-audit registration, in detail from the perspective of the auditor. This chapter guides companies through the registration audit step by step. Some of the information in this chapter is similar to that in Chapter 6, but it is written from the perspective of a company being audited. (This chapter assumes that a company has followed the preparation process outlined in Chapters 3 and 4, has had its documentation in place and its system operating for three to six months, and has held a series of internal audits.)

It is amazing that companies sometimes fail to prepare fully for the registration audit. For example, they fail to quiz their people on procedures or to test them on the mission statement. Frankly, this is naive. While it is certainly better to build a system with full participation of everyone, the implementation process simply does not always work that way, and when it doesn't, audit preparation becomes just like a final exam. You study hard to make sure you know the material, even if you have to stay up until 2:00 in the morning the day of the exam. The same is true of an audit. You should be completely prepared for it. Remember that the first audit is followed by the surveillance audit, so while you may cram for the first audit, full implementation and buy in must follow because the auditor will expect to see increasingly effective implementation of the system supported by documented evidence that the quality system is real rather than a "Potemkin Village" of procedures.

Be Auditor Friendly

One of the key points in making final preparations for the ISO/QS audit team's visit is to ensure that the company's quality system, its documentation, and its people are "auditor friendly." This means ensuring that the system is well organized; that processes are easy to trace; that documents are easy to find, easy to follow, and easy for someone from outside the company to read and understand; and that employees are well informed, friendly, helpful, and, most important, accessible to the auditor on reasonable notice. This is true of everyone in the company, from the CEO to the ISO champion to department heads to workers on the floor.

Although the audit is based on objective evidence, a company being audited must consider that the auditor is a human being, that his or her time at the company will be short, and that he or she will be busy the entire time. The auditor will not have a lot of time to search for documents, decipher illegible writing, or try to understand a convoluted procedure. If the records the auditor needs as evidence to prove compliance with a particular requirement cannot be found easily, he or she may assume that they do not exist. If the auditor cannot understand how a critical process works from the written procedures and process flow diagrams to which he or she has access and which he can easily find, the auditor may assume that no one else can and that the process does not work in accordance with the documentation. In each case, the auditor will probably give the company a nonconformance.

If the company CEO or the general manager of a large plant is too busy to meet with the auditor any time during the visit, the auditor will assume that the CEO or general manager does not pay much attention to the ISO or QS-9000 program and, therefore, the company's quality system probably does not comply with Clause 4.1, Management Responsibility. If company workers are sullen or noncommunicative, the auditor will assume that they—and the company—have something to hide and may dig deeper than originally intended. This is not to say that a company should try to influence the auditor's decisions. What it should do is make it easier for the auditor to do his or her job.

Make the Documentation System Easy to Understand

Chapters 3 and 4 cover ISO/QS-9000 implementation, including organizing the quality system and the supporting documentation. At this stage, the concern should be that the documentation system is easy for someone from the outside to understand. If the system was set up to meet the ISO requirements, it should already be auditor friendly. If, however, a company adapted an existing quality system to meet the ISO requirements, it must make sure that any information the ISO auditor needs can be easily found.

For example, suppose that under one company's quality system, documents pertaining to the calibration and maintenance of inspection, measuring, and test equipment (IMTE) are given a 200 series number (the overall policy for the section is 200, the first procedure is 210, the first work instruction under that procedure is 211, and so on). If the auditor cannot immediately grasp the documentation system (under ISO, IMTE is covered under Clause 4.11), he or she may assume that supporting documents do not exist. The same may be true if procedures and/or work instructions support more than one policy and are not cross-referenced. This problem can be eliminated by a simple cross-reference chart included in the main documentation files. By using it, the auditor will be able to find all the documentation needed. (Figure 7.1 shows a sample of such a chart.)

Compliance Matrix for ISO 9002

ISO Clause	4.1	4.2	4.3	4.4	4.5	4.6	4.7	4.8
Clause fulfilled by:			SOP 210 JWI 210 SOP 220 JWI 220 SOP 230 JWI 230	SOP 310 JWI 310 SOP 320 JWI 320 SOP 330	SOP 410 JWI 410 SOP 420 JWI 420 SOP 430 JWI 430 SOP 440 JWI 440 SOP 450 JWI 450 SOP 460 JWI 460 SOP 470 JWI 470 SOP 480 JWI 480	N/A	SOP 510 SOP 650 JWI 650 SOP 850 JWI 850 SOP 860 JWI 860 SOP 1210 JWI 1210 SOP 1220 JWI 1220 SOP 1230	SOP 610 JWI 610 SOP 620 JWI 620 SOP 630 JWI 630 SOP 640 JWI 640 SOP 650 JWI 650 SOP 660 JWI 660 SOP 670 JWI 670 SOP 680 JWI 680 SOP 690 JWI 690 SOP 700 JWI 700 SOP 720 JWI 720 SOP 730 JWI 730 SOP 740 JWI 740 SOP 850 JWI 850

The Registration Audit

4.9	4.10	4.11	4.12	4.13	4.14	4.15	4.16	4.17	4.18
SOP 810	SO 910	SOP 660	SOP 1010	SOP 1110	SOP 1210	SOP 1310	SOP 1410	SOP 1510	SOP 610
JWI 810	JWI 910	JWI 660	JWI 1010	JWI 1110	JWI 1210		JWI 1410		JWI 610
SOP 820	SOP 920	SOP 860	SOP 1020	SOP 1120	SOP 1220				
JWI 820		JWI 860		JWI 1120	JWI 1220				
SOP 830		SOP 860			SOP 1230				
JWI 830		SOP 1210		SOP 1410	JWI 1230				
SOP 840		JWI 1210		JWI 1410					
JWI 840		SOP 1220							
SOP 850		JWI 1220							
JWI 850									
SOP 860									
JWI 860									
SOP 1210									
JWI 1210									
SOP 1220									
JWI 1220									
SOP 1230									
JWI 1230									

Boxed areas indicate SOPs/JWIs with main applicability to another clause.

Figure 7.1 Compliance Matrix to Make Documentation Auditor-Friendly

A company must make sure that the documentation is written so that someone from outside the company can follow the procedures and work instructions. The documents should be written in clear language, not in company jargon that only a few insiders can understand. Of course, nearly all procedures will contain some terms that are unique to an industry or a company, but when the procedure is too encased in jargon, problems do occur. To ensure that procedures are understandable, a company should have people from outside the area try to follow a procedure. Bringing in people from sales to run a machine or complete the receiving process by following a written standard operating procedure, for example, is a great way to find out if that procedure is clearly written.

Think About It...

Can your company's documentation system be considered auditor friendly? If not, how would you make it so?

Prepare Employees

The auditors will typically interview several people in each ISO- or QS-9000-related function or department to see if written procedures and work instructions are being followed. They will also want to talk to certain people in each area to gain perspective on their respective operations. These people not only must be thoroughly trained in procedures and work instructions (see Chapter 4), but also must know how to react and talk to the auditors. It is a good idea for a company to hold a final preparation training session about a week before the auditors arrive. (As noted above, some people may object to this strategy. They believe that the auditors should find a company exactly as it is and the employees doing things just the way they always do them. In the author's experience, however, auditors expect companies to prepare for an audit, much as a teacher expects students to study and prepare for a test.)

The training, which should take about 30 minutes to an hour, should cover the basics of their procedures and the basics of auditing. The training should be conducted in mixed groups and should be instructive, fun, and just a bit competitive. The training should cover three areas:

1. **Purpose of the audit**—This includes what ISO/QS-9000 registration means, the steps a company has taken so far, and the importance of everyone being prepared.

2. ***Knowledge of mission statement, procedures, and work instructions***—The best way to cover this area is for the trainer to ask questions similar to those the auditor will ask. Examples include: "Does anyone from purchasing know what to do in case we need to get emergency approval of a vendor not on the approved vendor list?" "Does anyone from production know how we use statistical process control tools to monitor processes?" "Can someone from design outline our internal design approval process?" Another approach is to use a quiz such as the one in Table 7.1.
3. ***Preparation for an interview***—A company must be sure that employees know how to answer the auditors' questions accurately and completely without volunteering additional information. Table 7.2 shows ten things employees should know in preparing for the audit. In addition, it is a good idea to hold mock interviews, with one employee playing the role of the auditor and another the employee. The auditor should be working from a Quality System Assessment or other internal checklist.

Hold a Pre-Audit

The pre-audit has one purpose: to ensure that the auditee is ready for the registration audit. The effectiveness of this strategy is noted in one statistic: less than 20 percent of U.S. companies that did not have a pre-audit passed the ISO registration audit the first time. That figure jumps to over 80 percent for companies that had a pre-audit.

The pre-audit typically uncovers major systemic errors, gaps in the ISO/QS system, areas where compliance is marginal, lack of follow-through on procedures, employee and leadership complacence about the quality system, and other issues that can cause a company to fail the audit if they are not resolved before the registration auditors arrive. The pre-audit also provides a major psychological benefit to a company. After nonconformances noted in the pre-audit have been corrected, a company and its employees can approach the registration audit with far less apprehension. Employees who have been through a pre-audit feel that they can handle the actual audit and know that their system meets the intent of the standard. They are more relaxed and are not afraid to face the real audit. (*Note:* A few registration firms do not perform pre-audits. If the registration firm selected does not do a pre-audit, a company should have one done, under audit conditions, by a customer, a representative of a trade organization who has audit experience, or an outside consultant.)

Table 7.1 Sample ISO/QS-9000 Audit Preparation Quiz

1. If an auditor asks you a question and you do not know the answer, you should:
   a. Fake the answer; you probably know enough to convince the auditor.
   b. Just make a good guess.
   c. Change the subject to something you do know.
   d. Say something like, "I don't know, but I do know where to find the answer."
   e. Call your supervisor immediately.

2. Where (physically) are your procedures (the ones that apply directly to your job)? Write in the answer. _____
   _____

3. Auditors will typically want you to know any procedure that applies to your job word for word. ☐ True ☐ False

4. If an auditor asks you a specific question about a procedure that applies directly to your job, you should:
   a. Answer the question directly and specifically.
   b. Answer the question directly and specifically and add any other information that you think would better help the auditor understand the process.
   c. Try and guess what it is that the auditor really is asking and answer that.
   d. Explain that while the procedure says one thing, in your opinion, it is not always possible to follow this procedure. As a matter of fact, you know that some people hardly ever follow the procedure the way it is written.

5. Who maintains your procedures manual? (Write in the name of that individual.)

6. During an audit, the auditor will take time to look at every procedure in the company. ☐ True ☐ False

7. As long as you follow your procedures and tell an auditor that you do, that is sufficient evidence of compliance with the procedure. ☐ True ☐ False

8. It is okay to make an uncontrolled copy of a controlled document to keep in your desk so you are sure of what you are supposed to do. ☐ True ☐ False

9. In order to find the portion of a procedure that has changed in the latest revision, look for the little red arrow in the left margin of the procedure. ☐ True ☐ False

10. During the audit, the external auditor is always accompanied by a company escort. ☐ True ☐ False

11. If an auditor asks you a question about why you are doing a function that is consistent with basic procedures, the correct answer is:
    a. "I am following basic procedures."
    b. "I have worked here for 20 years, and I know my job."
    c. "I have been trained in my ISO procedures."

d. "When I came to the company, I got on-the-job training on how things were supposed to be done around here."
e. Combination of "a" and "c" above.

12. Auditors can be influenced by appearance, so it is important to keep your work area clean, your desk neat, the office clean and free of clutter, and otherwise present yourself and your department as well organized and ready to be audited. ☐ True ☐ False

13. If you disagree with a statement made by the auditor, the best thing to do is to argue. ☐ True ☐ False

14. It is okay to write a note on a procedure as long as you know that procedure is being revised and will be reissued soon. In this way, you let people know that a change is coming so that they can be prepared. ☐ True ☐ False

15. The following is a definition of an audit. Do you agree or disagree? If you disagree, write in why you disagree with this definition.

    An audit is an independent, systematic, and documented activity to evaluate, verify, and report on, by means of objective evidence, compliance with the requirements of a quality standard such as ISO 9000.

    ☐ Agree ☐ Disagree If you disagree, why? _____
    _____

16. What are the key points of the company quality mission statement?
    a. _____
    b. _____
    c. _____
    d. _____

17. How did you learn your procedures? _____
    _____

Answers

1. D
2. Write in
3. False
4. A
5. Write in
6. False
7. False
8. False (unless you have somehow written your procedure to allow this)
9. Company dependent
10. True
11. E
12. True
13. False
14. False
15. Agree
16. Write in
17. Write in something like, "I received training in my procedure."

Table 7.2 Ten Hints for Employees in Preparing for an Audit

1. Keep your desk as clean as possible. Clutter—(papers, manuals, etc.) gives the auditors more opportunity to ask questions.
2. Make sure you understand the question. Don't be afraid to ask the auditor to restate the question if you have any doubt about exactly what he or she means.
3. Answer the question directly. Don't waffle or bluff. This will merely give an auditor an opening for further questions.
4. Don't be afraid to admit that you don't know the answer to a question.
5. Don't give the auditor more information than he or she asks for. The more you tell, the greater the scope for the audit. Don't feel compelled to fill silence with words.
6. Know the procedures. The auditor may ask you to explain any and all procedures you follow in your job.
7. Be prepared. Think of the audit as a test. Make sure you are familiar with all aspects of your job.
8. Don't argue with the auditor. If you disagree with his or her conclusions, speak up, but make sure you are right before you do so.
9. Remain calm. It's easy to get defensive or rattled, but keep your cool. Any nervousness on your part may cause the auditor to detect a weakness and dig deeper.
10. Show you are committed to the company's quality process. The auditor will want to know that you believe what you are saying.

Either prior to the pre-audit or sometime before the registration audit, a company will be expected to provide a copy of its quality manual (at least the policies and usually examples of the procedures and work instructions) to the auditors. The auditors will examine this documentation to assure it meets the intended requirements of the ISO or QS standard and use it to plan exactly how they will proceed with the audit (what functions will be examined by which auditor, what questions will be asked, what methods will be used to gather evidence, and so on). If a company's quality manual contains any proprietary information (such as specific manufacturing technologies), the company can insist that proprietary information be examined only on-site.

There are two points worth noting here. First, it is important to ensure that any documentation given to the audit team is current. Second, the auditors may ask the person who gives them a document (usually the manager of quality assurance or the ISO champion) to explain the system used to keep documentation current. This person must be knowledgeable about the company's document control system. If this issue does not come up at this time, it almost certainly will come up later.

If the auditors' preliminary assessment turns up a considerable number of deficiencies in the company quality manual or if the manual is in disarray, the auditors can decide to postpone the registration audit until they deem that the company is ready. This was more common in the early days of ISO registration, when there were fewer models of what a quality manual should include and what it should look like. Today, companies have more examples available, so most have little trouble producing a quality manual that meets the intent of the standard.

Make Final Preparations

The time between the pre-audit and the actual assessment will be one of intense activity for a company. A company should remedy any nonconformances noted during the pre-audit (there almost certainly will be some) and should make a final assessment of all areas to ensure they are ready for the audit. A company should review all documentation to ensure that it is complete, current, and easy to locate. Specifically, this means going through the files to make sure they are accurate and up to date. At least two full days should be allowed for final preparation for the audit.

Just before the audit, a company should do a housekeeping check—ensure that all safety hazards are eliminated, all work areas are neat and organized (including employees' offices and desks), and the company exudes an aura of readiness. While neatness is not a requirement of ISO 9000, a well-organized and orderly workplace will convey the impression that a company "has its act together" and will help the auditors believe that a company's quality system is also well organized. If, on the other hand, the floors are dirty, employees' offices are untidy, and tool cabinets are in disarray, the auditors most likely will be influenced to believe that the quality system is also disorganized. No matter how organized a company is under the surface, it will have a hard time overcoming a negative first impression. A lot of little things, like product samples under a salesperson's desk or returned goods sitting unidentified on a warehouse shelf, can add up to a sense that a company is not really prepared for ISO/QS registration.

The Pre-Audit Meeting

Representatives of the auditing firm will ask to have an introductory meeting with company representatives (the ISO champion, the management representative, the CEO or president if available, and other key leaders). If there is no pre-assessment scheduled, the registrar will typically ask for a half-day on-site meeting. If there is a pre-audit, the activities listed below will usually be covered at that time. This meeting, which will be chaired by the lead auditor, has several purposes:

1. To introduce the auditors to the company and to learn from the company who the key company officials are
2. To acquaint the auditors with the company's audit representative(s), who will either escort them from department to department or site to site or will coordinate this activity (one of the representatives is generally the quality manager/ISO champion, but it can be anyone who is thoroughly familiar with both the company's operation and the purpose of the audit)
3. To set the details of the audit
4. To clear up any questions that the auditors may have about the quality manual submitted to them by the company
5. To establish a working relationship between the auditors and key company representatives

Introductions

The first thing the auditors will do is to introduce themselves and provide details about their backgrounds. Frequently, the details will include not only their auditing experience but also their prior work experience. For example,

> I am Jim McShane. I have been an auditor for six years with RMZ International and have been conducting ISO audits since 1989. Before that, I was auditing to the GMP standards. I am a certified quality auditor. I am a graduate chemical engineer with a master's degree in business. I started my career as a chemist with Dorm Chemicals, have managed labs, and have been an assistant plant manager for five years with Mitvaco.

If an auditor does not volunteer this information, a company has a right to ask for it.

The Registration Audit **163**

A good percentage of the auditors who are conducting ISO/QS audits today have technical degrees. A company should determine if this technical degree qualifies the auditor to assess its operation. Does a background in engineering prepare an auditor for the evaluation of a large distribution company or an accounting firm? If an auditor has experience as a chief engineer on an oceangoing vessel, is he or she prepared for the quality problems facing the traffic manager of a marine transportation company that plies the Mississippi from St. Louis to Baton Rouge? While the answer to this question is most likely yes, it is important that a company find out about the auditor's personal scope.

It is of critical importance that the auditor have some understanding of the basic nature of the business in which a company is involved. A company should ask questions to ensure that the auditor does have this knowledge. Although it is, for obvious reasons, very rarely done, a company has the right to reject an auditor if that auditor does not have a background that would provide at least a broad understanding of the company's business.

The company representatives should also introduce themselves and give the auditors some basic information about themselves and about the company. This information should include the products manufactured and/or the services provided, the equipment used, and any other standards to which the company is registered.

Details About the Audit

A company should provide the auditors with a layout of the facility showing departments, production lines, and other key areas. If the auditors give advance notice of the areas that will be included in the audit, the company should mark those areas. The auditors and the company will confirm the dates of the registration audit and will determine the details as follows:

1. **Will the entire facility be included in the audit?**—If not, which departments will be involved? If a company is going to exclude some functions from the audit (either for separate registration or because it does not wish to register those functions), company leaders should ensure that the auditors know this. A company also should tell the auditors about shift starting times and days (five eight-hour days, four ten-hours days, etc.).
2. **What criteria will be used in the audit?**—A company has already decided to which ISO standard it wishes to become registered, but

it should discuss any exceptions at this time. For example, a company that has no design function but does servicing would register under ISO 9001, but Clause 4.4, Design Control, would be excluded from the audit. (If a company does design but not servicing, Clause 4.19 would be excluded.) For a QS-9000 audit, details as to the organization of the audit will be clarified.

3. *How will the audit be conducted?*—The auditor will tell a company about the methods to be used in gathering evidence during the audit (observing, sampling, tracing, and interviewing) and if the auditors will be deployed individually or in groups. The auditor and company representatives will determine if the audit is to be conducted by ISO 9001 paragraph (e.g., the auditors would check document control procedures in each department [Clause 4.5] and then check purchasing procedures [Clause 4.6]) or by department (e.g., one auditor would examine production, checking for compliance with all applicable requirements, while another assesses purchasing). The auditors also will discuss briefly what will constitute a nonconformance, how nonconformances will be documented, and what the consequences will be (how many nonconformances must be found before a company is considered to have failed the audit). This is very important because the pass–fail system can vary according to where the primary registry agency is located (the United States, United Kingdom, Netherlands, etc.) and other factors.

4. *What support does the audit team need during the visit?*—The auditors will tell a company what they will need during the audit—accommodations, meals, meeting room, telephone, etc. (At one time, it was common for auditors to request secretarial assistance, but most auditors today carry notebook computers.) A company should inform the auditors of any special security or safety requirements (passes, hard hats) as well as any special circumstances. For example, if a number of employees speak a language other than English, the company should tell the auditors to ensure that at least one member of the audit team can communicate with workers.

At this time, the auditors will bring up any questions they have about the company quality manual (policies, procedures, and work instructions). If the company's manual is well organized, the auditors may have no questions or will only need to clear up minor misunderstandings.

Company representatives should be able to clear up any misunderstandings; they should also provide the auditors with any changes or additions that have been made since the manual was given to the auditors (possibly as a result of the pre-audit). If Items 1 to 4 above are not covered in the pre-meeting, company representatives should raise the issues and assure they know the answers.

Think About It...

Suppose representatives of an auditing firm are meeting with you to discuss an ISO/QS audit at your company. What special circumstances would you need to tell them about? What special arrangements would you have to make to accommodate the auditors?

Establish a Relationship

A key function of the preliminary meeting is to allow the auditors to establish a working relationship with company representatives. A company naturally will be somewhat apprehensive about an audit, and some representatives may even resent the "intrusion" by the auditors. Company representatives should be open to the auditors during the pre-audit and should exude a spirit of cooperation and a willingness to work with the auditors. They will find that this cooperation is generally reciprocated. If, on the other hand, company representatives show resentment toward the auditors, they will find that the resentment may be reciprocated and the assessment may be more difficult than necessary.

The Registration Audit

The registration audit starts with another brief meeting between the members of the audit team and representatives of the company (the ISO champion, the CEO, and a few other key leaders). The main purpose of this meeting is to set the agenda for the audit. Because of time constraints (audits usually last two days, with audits of very large companies sometimes taking three to five days), the auditors will not be able to examine every single process in a company. Instead, they will examine what is known as a "vertical slice," a narrow band of processes and documentation stretching across department lines. The vertical slice technique is used by nearly all auditors. While it narrows the picture the auditors will get of a company, it also provides the auditors the opportunity to look at some functions in depth rather than looking at all functions on a cursory basis.

During the opening meeting, the audit team will typically explain what specific areas of the company will be examined. The team will stick

ISO 9001 Assessment

Company: GKI
Site: Corporate Headquarters
Date: September 16, 1996

Day One

Time	Auditor 1	Auditor 2
8:30–9 a.m.	**Opening Meeting** Don Wall, Jane Thore	
9–10:30 a.m.	**Management** Don Wall Jane Thore Lynn Calkins Bob Rouser	**Maintenance and Repair** Rick Stinson Dick Garrison Don Ingram Debbie Hooper Jerry Byerly M&R staff
10:30–Noon	**Sales** Robin Wilson David Bishop Lu Ann Jackson Sales representatives Sales secretaries	
Noon–1 p.m.	**Lunch** Auditors, Don Wall, Jane Thore	
1–4 p.m.	**Shipping** Bill Sebastian Sharon Ware Fleet managers Dispatchers	**Purchasing** Rick Stinson Darryl Lawson
4–4:30 p.m.	**Auditor Review Meeting** Auditors	

Figure 7.2 Agenda for ISO Audit

The Registration Audit

to these areas unless it finds evidence of nonconformances that require more investigation, in which case the team will broaden its scope.

Generally, the audit team will establish a tentative agenda as part of its preparations for the audit. The lead auditor usually will convey this tentative agenda to the company's ISO champion a few days before the audit is to begin. At the initial meeting, the company will suggest any changes that should be made to the agenda. For example, if a production line that was scheduled to be audited the first day had to be shut down for emergency maintenance, the audit of that area would be postponed until the second day of the audit. (Figure 7.2 shows an agenda for an ISO audit; it would not differ significantly for a QS-9000 audit except for the obvious addition of the QS-9000 requirements.)

ISO 9001 Assessment

Company: GKI
Site: Corporate Headquarters
Date: September 16, 1996

Day Two

Time	Auditor 1	Auditor 2
8:30–9 a.m.	**Auditor/Client Meeting**	Ron Crump, Jane Thore
9–Noon	**Purchasing** Ron Crump Jane Thore Jerry McDaniel	**Production** Yank Cooper Randall McPherson
Noon–1 p.m.	**Lunch** Jane Thore, Ron Crump	
1–3:30 p.m.	**Inspection & Testing** Ron Crump Jane Thore Katherine Smart	**Production-Calibration** Dianne Matthews Kevin McGee
4–4:30 p.m.	**Personnel** Nancy Everett Marilyn Welch	**Training** Barbara Ransom Mary Blake
4:30–5:30 p.m.	**Final Meeting** Auditors, Jane Thore, Don Wall, Rick Stinson, Ron Crump	

Figure 7.2   Agenda for ISO Audit (continued)

A company should have identified contacts and/or escorts for the auditors from each department or area. The auditors should never be given free reign in a facility. They should always be escorted. The ISO champion should introduce the escorts to the audit team at this meeting and should also distribute any security passes or safety equipment such as hard hats or safety glasses (one shipping firm issued lifejackets to audit team members who were scheduled to inspect its craft).

This meeting also is the time to settle any logistical details. The ISO champion should show audit team members to the meeting room they will be using during the audit, give them any special instructions about using the telephone, and point out other key facilities such as break rooms or rest rooms. At this point, the auditors will go about the business of the audit.

Visit with the CEO

In most cases, the first thing one of the auditors (usually the lead auditor) will want to do is meet directly with the CEO or senior executive of the facility. The purpose of this meeting is to assess the CEO's involvement with the ISO/QS program in accordance with Clause 4.1, Management Responsibility. The auditor will ask the CEO questions about the ISO program, much the same way other auditors will interview other people in the company. This meeting is critical. While management responsibility is only one of 20 requirements of ISO 9001 and signs of true top management involvement will not guarantee passage of the audit, indications that the CEO is not heavily involved with, or at least knowledgeable and supportive of, the ISO program almost surely will cause a company to receive a major nonconformance and may cause it to fail the audit. The CEO must not be too busy to see the auditor. (In the case of a legitimate emergency, the CEO should appoint, in writing, the second highest ranking official in the company to act in his or her stead.) As with all other employees, the most senior member of the company at the location (CEO, plant manager, district manager, regional vice president, branch manager, etc.) should be well prepared for the audit. Special quizzes on management responsibility and the quality system are often given to these senior leaders to prepare them for the audit.

Conducting the Audit

The auditors will typically come prepared with checklists for each department or area of the company to be audited. These checklists are de-

The Registration Audit

signed to help the auditor examine a company's compliance with its written policies, procedures, and work instructions. The auditors will show these checklists to company representatives at the initial meeting, so the company knows exactly which functions the auditors will be examining. The checklists generally consist of very narrow yes or no questions (e.g., "Does inspection, measuring, and test equipment show signs of calibration at intervals required by Policy 4.11(b)?"), along with a space for comments or evidence of compliance or noncompliance. Table 7.3 shows a list of the things auditors typically look for in each area of ISO compliance.

Table 7.3   Things Auditors Look for in Each Area of ISO Compliance

Clause 4.1 Management Responsibility
- Top management supports and is involved in quality and ISO policies.
- Management is knowledgeable of the content of quality policies.
- Top management (CEO) assumes responsibility for quality in the company.
- Quality responsibilities and authorities are clearly defined.
- Internal auditors are independent of function being audited.
- Member of company's own management is involved in the process.

Clause 4.2 Quality System
- The company has a quality manual describing the quality system.
- The company's documentation system is based on and is in compliance with the ISO requirements.
- All employees have knowledge of the quality system appropriate to their level in the organization and their job responsibilities.
- Quality planning.

Clause 4.3 Contract Review
- All contracts are reviewed to see that they comply with requirements.
- Contracts include identified quality-relevant factors.
- Procedures in production and other areas all the company meet the contract requirements.
- The company maintains records of contract reviews.

Clause 4.4 Design Control
- Design procedures exist and are in compliance with the standard.
- Design plans identify all required elements.
- Design input and output requirements are identified.
- Designs, including modifications, show evidence of review and approval by appropriate people.

Clause 4.5 Document and Data Control
- All quality documents, and amendments, show evidence of review and approval.
- Company has systems to verify, approve, distribute, and maintain documents.
- Company maintains master list of current documents.

Table 7.3 Things Auditors Look for in Each Area of ISO Compliance (continued)

Clause 4.6 Purchasing
- Company maintains approved vendor list.
- Vendors are selected based on ability to satisfy requirements, and that ability is monitored using specified assessment criteria.
- Company inspects and/or tests incoming products (if the company uses other methods, such as charts, etc., supplied by a vendor, those records must be maintained).
- Purchasing documents are complete, accurate, and current.

Clause 4.7 Customer-Supplied Product
- Products supplied by purchaser (customer) are stored and handled properly.
- Nonconforming products are segregated, and customer knows of their condition.

Clause 4.8 Product Identification and Traceability
- Products are identified throughout production.
- Identification of product is appropriate to product type.

Clause 4.9 Process Control
- Process requirements are defined in company's documentation.
- Production processes are approved by appropriate authority.
- Special processes are monitored and controlled.
- Production personnel meet appropriate requirements.

Clause 4.10 Inspection and Testing
- Incoming materials are inspected and/or tested.
- In-process materials are inspected and/or tested.
- Final products are inspected and/or tested before being released for delivery.
- Inspection and testing procedures are accurate, complete, and current.
- Inspection and test records are accurate, complete, current, and available for review.

Clause 4.11 Inspection, Measuring, and Test Equipment (IMTE)
- All IMTE is controlled.
- Company has policies and procedures to ensure reliability and accuracy of IMTE.
- IMTE is referenced to national and international standards.

Clause 4.12 Inspection and Test Status
- Inspection and test status of all products is identified.
- Inspection status records are accurate, complete, and current.

Clause 4.13 Control of Nonconforming Product
- Nonconforming products are clearly identified and segregated.
- Company has policies and procedures for reworking, accepting, or scrapping nonconforming product.
- Rejected products are disposed of properly.

Table 7.3   Things Auditors Look for in Each Area of ISO Compliance (continued)

Clause 4.14 Corrective and Preventive Action
- Company has policies and procedures for determining causes of nonconforming products.
- Preventive measures are instituted to eliminate nonconformances and keep them from recurring.
- Company monitors effectiveness of corrective action.

Clause 4.15 Handling, Storage, Packaging and Delivery
- Internal movements of products are identified.
- Company has policies and procedures to minimize damage during handling, storage, packaging, and delivery.
- Company assesses effectiveness of packaging.
- Materials are protected during delivery.

Clause 4.16 Quality Records
- Records are properly identified, maintained, filed, and indexed.
- Persons responsible for maintaining records are identified.
- Records can be traced to a product or process.
- Records are "readily retrievable."

Clause 4.17 Internal Quality Audits
- Comprehensive internal audits are scheduled on a regular and appropriate basis.
- Auditors are qualified.
- Audits follow an identifiable process which includes planning, corrective action, and reporting.
- Auditors use checklists that reflect customer and other requirements.
- Effectiveness of corrective action is monitored.

Clause 4.18 Training
- Training needs are assessed on a regular and appropriate basis.
- Training personnel meet appropriate qualifications.
- Training records are accurate, complete, current, and available.

Clause 4.19 Servicing
- Servicing meets customer requirements.
- Servicing scope is identified.

Clause 4.20 Statistical Techniques
- Appropriate statistical techniques are used as required.
- Company analyzes effectiveness of statistical techniques.

Source: Survey of ISO auditors conducted by the author, along with observations of audits of client companies.

The auditors will follow their checklists as written, unless some objective evidence suggests the need to explore an issue in greater depth. If they must invest more time in a given area than was planned in order to investigate potential discrepancies, they will have to compensate somewhere else. For a company's first audit, the auditor is mainly interested in ensuring that the company has a quality system that meets the intent of the standards and is operational. In later audits, the auditor will look for more evidence of operational effectiveness. The audits will generally become more rigorous as a company's quality system matures.

The company representative who will be escorting the auditor through a particular area probably will be able to follow the progress of the audit by observing the auditor's checklist. If the company representative has any questions about how the company is faring or any information the auditor writes on the checklist, he or she should ask the auditor. Most audits are conducted with a policy of "no secrets," and the auditor will share any information with the company representative.

Gathering Evidence

The auditors use four basic methods of gathering evidence during the audit: observation, tracing, sampling, and interviewing. Observation means just that—the auditor looks around to see what he or she can see. In many cases, evidence of compliance or noncompliance will be easy to spot. For example, the auditor should be able to tell just by looking if nonconforming material is segregated properly. The auditor can look at tags on test equipment to see if it has been calibrated at the specified intervals or can watch a worker on the second shift to see if he or she follows the same procedures as workers on the first shift.

Tracing means following a process from beginning to end (or sometimes from end to beginning). The auditor can trace the production of a particular item or the path of an order from inside sales to shipping. The auditor will start by examining the documentation to learn the way the process is supposed to work and then will follow one item through the process to see if it does, indeed, work that way.

Sampling

Sampling is one of the most effective and most common methods of gathering evidence during an audit. Sampling is the process of examining a number of examples of a product or documents and extrapolating the findings to get a picture of the whole. There are four advantages to sampling: (1) the sample size can be determined in advance; (2) the result can be compared to 100 percent examination; (3) sampling conserves time; and (4) the result is unbiased, defensible, and objective and can be reasonably duplicated by another auditor, the company representative, or anyone else.

The auditor will not be able to sample every single process or type of documentation in the quality system. Therefore, he or she generally will sample only crucial items. The auditor will have determined which items he or she wants to sample by studying the company's documentation beforehand. The auditor's observations or interviews with company workers also may suggest areas for sampling. Areas likely to be sampled include points where two processes meet or where responsibility for a process passes from one organization to another; new processes, which involve a learning curve; processes that are overloaded or where there are not enough people to ensure proper controls; processes that have a history of inefficiencies or defects; and processes for purchasing, document control, corrective action, and records management.

The size of the sample will vary, depending on the size of the population (the number of items that exist), the nature of the process being sampled, and the confidence factor the auditor wishes to reach. Most auditors will take about 50 samples at random from each process. (Sampling is covered in full in Chapter 6.)

As the company representative watches the auditor conduct the sampling, he or she may be tempted to help the auditor select samples. The company representative must resist this temptation. The auditor will typically insist on selecting his or her own samples. Even if the company representative is merely trying to be helpful, the auditor will think he or she is trying to steer him or her to samples that will reflect positively on the company. Any "help" from the company representative will be viewed negatively and may cause the auditor to dig a little deeper than he or she normally would. Of course, if an auditor asks you to pull samples for review, do so.

When the auditor has finished sampling, he or she will tell the company representative of the findings. This normally will be expressed as a probability of a percentage of defects or nonconformities, known as the confidence factor. For example, the auditor might say, "I am 95 percent confident that no more than 9 percent of products (or documents) are nonconforming" or "I am 95 percent confident that the compliance factor is at least 91 percent."

Think About It...

If an auditor were conducting an audit of your department, what process would he or she be most likely to sample?

Interviewing

The auditor will conduct numerous interviews with workers in each area of the company, both individually and in groups. Some of the interviews will be brief, only one or two questions, and will be done on the spot. Others will take some time, and the company should provide the auditor with a quiet place to conduct the interviews. Generally, the auditor will tell the company representative in advance that he or she wants to interview a certain number of people in each area of the company. The auditor will choose the people to be interviewed; as in sampling, the company representative should not offer to "help." However, if the auditor asks the company representative who to talk to about a certain procedure, the company representative should provide the name of a person to be interviewed. Again, use judgment here; choose someone who is familiar with the process and procedures, not the newest employee or someone who wants to "send a message" to management.

Preparing Employees for Interviews

Many employees may be nervous about being interviewed by the auditors, especially those employees for whom public speaking or presentations are not normally part of the job. They may be confused about exactly what the audit means to the company and to them, or they may be concerned about reprisals if they "spill the beans." As noted earlier, company leaders should ensure that employees thoroughly understand the written procedures, that they follow them, and that they know how to explain them to the auditor. Company leaders should assure employees that there will be no reprisals for answers that may reflect badly on the company, as long as those answers are well informed, truthful, and in direct response to questions asked. In smaller companies or remote locations, practicing the interview process with employees is a good idea. The quality manager, ISO/QS champion, or another employee should play the role of auditor and actually conduct a practice interview.

Handling the Interview

Employees should know that they will be asked how they do a particular task and that their answers will be compared to written procedures and work instructions. They will be asked to explain how the processes with which they should be familiar work. Employees also should be prepared to explain how corrective action is implemented when "normal systems" fail to operate "normally." They should expect the auditors to ask what happens when the volume of work exceeds the volume that full-time staffing was designed to handle or when other irregularities put intense pressure on the staff and facilities.

Employees should know that the auditor will ask mostly open-ended questions, that is, questions that require more than a yes or no answer. Examples include: "When you first start to put the frame together, what is the first step?" "After you take the customer's information, what do you do with the order form?" "Where does the assembly go after you have attached the framistan?" The auditor will continue to ask questions until he or she gets a complete answer: "What is the next step?" "Then what happens?" When the employee has finished answering, the auditor may ask a direct, or closed, question: "At that point, are you finished with your part of the operation?"

It is not unusual for an auditor to ask an employee to take the auditor through a specific procedure step by step, including providing evidence of compliance in the policy documentation.

Employees should be coached to give complete, honest, open answers to each question the auditor asks. However, they should also know not to volunteer information. For example, if the auditor asks, "When you are finished with your part of the subassembly, to whom do you pass it?" The employee should answer truthfully but should avoid saying, "Well, now I pass it to Joe Smith, but before we had established procedures, I just set it aside and someone would pick it up."

As the interview progresses, the auditor probably will "write out loud." That is, the auditor will read any notes as he or she writes them and ask if that is indeed what the employee really meant. Employees should know that this requires a "yes" or a "no" and is not a request for additional information.

Employees should know that the most common error made in audit interviews is *giving too much information to the auditor*. In one case, an auditor was conducting an audit of a piece of equipment that depended upon the accuracy of a magnetic compass. When the auditor asked the operator about the equipment, he replied that it did work but that "even a minor intrusion of metal influences the compass, so I have done a series of calculations to overcome the effects of the intrusion. So I know if...then I...." This was, of course, a nonconformance. The operator's calculations were not part of the written procedures. If the operator were absent, serious consequences could arise. The operator should have explained the need to do these calculations during the writing of the procedure, not during the audit. The finding also hurt the company in that it made the auditor question what else is being hidden and thus increased the intensity of the audit. The root cause of this nonconformance is the malfunctioning compass. Explaining it away simply made the nonconformance worse.

Think About It...

Suppose you are being interviewed as part of an audit of your company. What questions would you expect the auditor to ask you? How would you answer them?

After the Interview

When the interview is completed, the auditor will share any tentative conclusions he or she has drawn with the employee. If the auditor's initial analysis indicates that the system is working as it should, the auditor will let the employee know that he or she has done well. If, on the other hand, there seems to be a discrepancy, or if the employee has given an answer that seems to contradict information gathered from sampling, observation, or previous interviews, the auditor will make an effort to reconcile the two versions.

The auditor then will tell the employee what the next step is. If the auditor has gotten all the information needed from the employee, he or she will tell the employee so, emphasizing that the employee has done a good job and the interview is finished. If, however, the auditor thinks the employee has more information that may be helpful but cannot continue the interview because of another appointment or because he or she needs to check some facts before asking any more questions, the auditor will make an appointment to return at a later time.

Corroborating

As discussed in Chapter 6, in all evidence gathering, the auditors will look for evidence that corroborates (confirms or backs up) the documented system or evidence that corroborates the conclusion that the systems is not working properly. Frequently, one auditor will find some evidence of a nonconformance in one area of a department, while another auditor will find corroborating evidence in another area. When they compare notes, they discover that a nonconformance exists. For example, suppose a sales order for a particular customer shows that the customer ordered 250 brake drums. However, the shipping log shows that 180 were shipped. There is no paperwork to show that the order was changed. This is evidence of a nonconformance; it will also result in further digging to see if it is a pattern or an exception.

Sharing Information

As stated earlier, the auditors generally will share any information they find or any conclusions they develop with company representatives who escort them through the various areas of the company. At the end of each day of the audit, the auditors will meet to discuss the findings of the day and any corroborating evidence. They also will study the next day's agenda to see if it needs to be altered to accommodate any further fact finding necessitated by the first day's findings.

The lead auditor will then meet with a company's ISO champion (or another representative) to inform him or her of what the team has learned, what it means, and how the audit is progressing. The lead auditor also will answer any questions the ISO champion has about the conduct of the audit or the results gathered so far. The lead auditor will provide information on any changes in the agenda and note any needs the audit team has. The ISO champion should try to accommodate any requests the audit team makes. If, however, a request is impossible to meet (e.g., the lead auditor requests another meeting with the CEO, who has just left on an urgent business trip), the two should discuss alternatives and reach a compromise. The lead auditor will accept a reasonable explanation for the company's inability to meet his or her request. (In this case, a phone interview might substitute.)

Nonconformances

During the audit, the auditors will disclose any nonconformances they find to the company representative for the department and to the ISO champion, usually on a nonconformance report (NCR). (Figure 7.3 shows a sample nonconformance report.) This report will contain:

1. Formatting or labeling that clearly links the report to the audit from which it resulted
2. Details on what was observed or identified as being deficient
3. Identification of the nonconformance as major or minor/Category 1 or Category 2
4. The reasons why the deficiency is a major or a minor nonconformance
5. The time and place the observation was made
6. The persons involved at the time of the discovery
7. The type of evidence that will be needed to verify that the nonconformance has been corrected

The classification of a nonconformance as major or minor (or, in the case of some registrars, Category 1 or Category 2) usually is based on the auditor's judgment of the potential consequences of failing to correct it, on how often the nonconformance was noticed, and on whether the nonconformance is judged to be systemic or random and isolated.

Major Nonconformances

As the name implies, major nonconformances represent serious deviations from the standards. They include policies or procedures that do not meet the intent of the ISO standards, whose results do not comply with the requirements, or that are ignored by the work force or are seriously altered in actual use. A very large number of minor nonconformances in a given operating area can also constitute a major nonconformance. Examples of major nonconformances include the following:

- Lack of a procedure to approve vendors
- No procedure in place to assure that contracts are properly reviewed
- Falsification of any record

M-LULTD.Quality Audits Company: GKI Audit Date: 8-2-96 NCR No.: 96-08-A7	**Nonconformance** **Report**

Department and Subject Audited: Production
Auditors: Bill Frame (Lead)   John Olin
QA Standard Applied: ISO 9002   Section 4.5   Document Control
Type of Nonconformance: Category 1 _____   Category 2 __X__
Nonconformance(s) Noted: 1. Installers were using obsolete revisions of standard operating procedures.   2. The nature of changes to controlled documents in the production area are not clearly identified.
Signature: _____   Signature: _____   (Company Representative)   (Lead Auditor)
Corrective Action Verified: **CAR Close-out Date:**   8-8-96   Signature: _____   (Lead Auditor)

Figure 7.3 Sample Nonconformance Report

- Lack of calibration data for critical measurement equipment (this could be major or minor, depending on the auditor and how widespread the problem is—systemic or random and isolated)
- Lack of training records
- Uncontrolled copies of controlled documents in use in a department (usually made by employees for their own use, but still a nonconformance)

Major nonconformances require serious effort on the part of a company to remedy. If, for example, policies or procedures do not meet the intent of the standard, they will have to be rewritten and the entire work force trained in the new version. If employees are not using existing procedures, a company will have to examine them to see if they are appropriate. If not, they will have to be rewritten. If they are appropriate but are just being ignored by employees, a company will have to train employees thoroughly in the procedures and may even have to impose sanctions to make the employees follow the proper procedures.

If the auditor considers the nonconformance serious enough, a company may have to undergo a reaudit of the area affected. If a company receives a large number of nonconformances, it may even have to undergo a complete reaudit. In either case, the registration process will be delayed.

Minor Nonconformances

Minor nonconformances are not as serious in their potential consequences, but neither are they frivolous. They usually are the slight differences between desired practices or outcomes and those that are actually observed. In some cases, minor nonconformances are the result of miscommunication and can be cleared up on the spot. Others may require specific corrective action that will not be completed until the audit team has left. Examples of minor nonconformances include the following:

- One piece of equipment missing a calibration date (if all similar equipment is properly tagged)
- One part of the training records missing
- Two documents out of 60 samples with an incorrect date
- Two items out of 50 samples past the expiration date
- One individual who fails to follow a job work instruction
- Some employees who do not know or understand the quality policy statement (depending on the number, this could be major or minor)

It is important to remember that what constitutes a major nonconformance and what constitutes a minor nonconformance can vary depending on the auditor, the frequency of the nonconformance, and the critical or noncritical nature of the area in which the nonconformance is found. (Figure 7.4 shows the types of nonconformances found in ISO audits and the frequency of each type.)

The Registration Audit 181

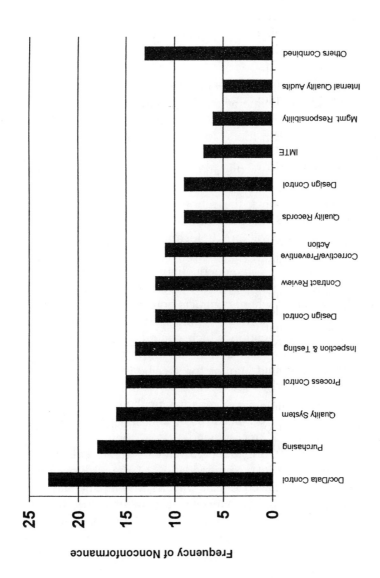

Figure 7.4 ISO Nonconformance Notices by Category

Final Meeting

When their auditors have finished their assessment of a company, they will hold a final meeting with company representatives. This meeting involves the full audit team and the same company representatives who attended the initial meeting. Company executives, including the CEO, should also attend this meeting.

The lead auditor will present a report on the audit team's activities. He or she will spend some time at the beginning of the meeting briefly relating the methods used in conducting the audit and talking about the positive things the audit team found (the things that were in compliance with the requirements). Then the lead auditor will give a summary of the nonconformances found during the audit (most of which company representatives should already know).

Because of time constraints, the report will, of course, be in rough form, but it will contain all the findings (evidence of nonconformances) of the audit. The auditors will not hold anything back for the formal written report. The report will not contain all the details of the findings but instead will concentrate on generic findings and conclusions. For example, the lead auditor may say, "The audit team found 10 separate instances out of 50 samples where contracts bore no signs of review. This indicates a serious problem with the contract review process." The lead auditor probably will not mention which contracts were in noncompliance. However, a company has a right to know the details; the ISO champion should ask the lead auditor for specific evidence if he or she so desires.

The report will also include a company's final "grade" on the audit. There are typically three possibilities: pass, fail, and provisional. "Pass" means that the auditor will recommend that a company receive ISO registration immediately. (Only the registrar can grant registration, although it usually follows the recommendation of the auditor, after the audit report has been reviewed.) "Fail" means a company has such a large number of major nonconformances (the number varies from auditing firm to auditing firm) or the nonconformance or nonconformances found are of such a serious nature that the company will have to remedy the nonconformances and then undergo another complete audit. "Provisional" is by far the most common outcome. It means that a company's quality system is generally operating well and according to the standards, but there are some points that need to be addressed before actual registration can be granted. For some auditing firms today, the process is really best described as "pass/pass." A company will be reaudited as necessary until it passes the audit.

As a practical matter, no auditing agency makes it a point to fail 100 percent of the organizations it audits. To do so would severely limit the number of applications it could anticipate in the future. A similar result would arise if a registrar had a 100 percent first-time registration rate over a significant period of time, because its credibility or professionalism might be questioned.

Receiving Bad News Well

If the auditors have found a considerable number and variety of nonconformances, the final meeting may not be very pleasant for company representatives. After all, they have to listen to a list of their company's shortcomings. Company representatives should try to accept the bad news in the spirit in which it is offered—as an opportunity for improvement or a way to enhance their company's processes. They should not take offense at the lead auditor or members of the team who reported the nonconformances; this is, after all, their function. The nonconformances existed, and the auditors reported them; they did not make them up. Company representatives should not take an "us versus them" attitude toward the auditors. Nor should they argue with the lead auditor or members of the team. Arguing generally will make the auditors more adamant in their conclusions. (It is important to remember that the auditors will conduct surveillance audits every six months or so for the term of the registration, which is usually three years.)

If, however, a nonconformance resulted from a minor misunderstanding on the part of the auditor or a failure to explain the process correctly on the part of someone from the company, company representatives should attempt to clear up this point at this time. If the company's explanation is valid, the auditors usually will consider the matter settled, and the nonconformance either will not be listed on the final report or will be listed as having been remedied.

Company representatives also should not take a "so what" attitude toward the findings of the audit. While some of the findings may seem trivial, they should all be considered serious for two reasons: because a company will not receive ISO registration until they are remedied and because the nonconformances hurt a company's total quality and thus its bottom line.

While the lead auditor will tell a company what nonconformances need to be remedied and what evidence will be accepted as proof that they have been remedied, he or she will not give any specific recommendations as to how to go about remedying the nonconformances. This practice has developed over the history of the audit process. Auditors have learned that if they make a specific recommendation, a company will invariably take the recommendation to mean "you must do it this way" or "if you do it this way, I guarantee you'll pass the audit," which may not be the case. A company must determine its own course of corrective action, based on the auditor's findings and the company's own quality system.

Once the auditors have presented their findings and a company has had a chance to respond, the lead auditor will end the meeting. The two sides will then go to the next stages—for the auditor, writing the final report, and for the company, determining what corrective actions are needed and implementing them.

The Final Report

About two weeks after the end of the audit (sometimes less), the audit team will send the company a final written report on the results of the audit. This written report will contain the same information presented in the oral report; however, if a company has remedied a nonconformance in the period between the oral report and the final report, that will be noted in the final report.

The report will begin with a summary of exactly how the function is operating. The summary will include areas that are functioning well, as well as areas in which nonconformances were noted and improvement is needed.

The body of the report will detail the nonconformances and the evidence that supports them, as well as the evidence the lead auditor will accept as proof that the nonconformances have been remedied. In the case of very minor nonconformances, the lead auditor may require only that a company state what it is doing to remedy them. For more serious, but still relatively minor nonconformances, the lead auditor probably will want to see documentation proving that the corrective actions have been initiated and that they are working. For major nonconformances, the lead auditor may insist upon a reaudit of the function involved. All this will be spelled out in the final report.

The final report will be sent to the ISO/QS champion (or other designated company representative), who should distribute copies of the report to company executives and to the heads of all areas affected. The ISO steering committee should meet to plan and write the company's response to the report. The response, which should be filed within 30 days of receiving the final report, will detail the company's plan for corrective action.

Corrective Action

A company should start planning corrective action as soon as possible after the auditors leave the facility following the audit. A company should not wait for the final report; the sooner the nonconformances are remedied, the sooner a company will receive ISO/QS registration.

The ISO steering committee should meet with the heads of the departments in which nonconformances were cited to plan the corrective actions. Three steps should be taken: (1) find the problem, (2) find the root cause of the problem, and (3) fix the root cause of the problem. The first step already has been done—the nonconformances are the problems.

Finding the Root Cause of the Problems

Like a disease, a quality problem has both symptoms and causes. The nonconformance cited in the audit is only the symptom; treating it will make the company look better on the surface, but unless the cause is treated, the nonconformance (or a similar one) will recur.

For example, consider a company that was cited for a document control nonconformance because certain documents did not bear signatures indicating that they were reviewed as called for in the company's procedures. If the appropriate person reviews and signs the documents after the nonconformance is noticed, that eliminates the symptom, but it is a sure bet that the problem will crop up again. Similarly, a harsh memo from the CEO stating that all documents will be reviewed and signed in the future may eliminate some recurrences, but it will not stop all of them because the cause of the problem has not been addressed. To eliminate the problem, the company must first find out why the documents were not reviewed and signed. Then, and only then, can the problem be solved.

Fishbone Analysis

One of the best ways to determine the root cause of a problem is through a statistical process control (SPC) tool known as a fishbone or Ishikawa diagram. This tool is used in brainstorming sessions to search for the cause of a problem. It is known as a fishbone for obvious reasons—it looks like the outline of a fish skeleton. The problem to be studied constitutes the head of the fish, and the "backbone" stretches back to the tail. Six "ribs" branch out from the backbone to form the "skeleton" of the fish. These ribs are labeled *Machinery, Methods, Measurement, Material, People,* and *Environment.* (Figure 7.5 shows an example of a fishbone diagram.)

The fishbone diagram is most effective when used in a group of five or six people closest to the process. One member of the team acts as the facilitator. When someone comes up with an idea, the facilitator draws a "bone" off the appropriate "rib" and writes the suggestion down. In some cases, an item can appear on more than one rib. In the example below, the policy requiring that contracts be reviewed by a certain person could be placed under "Methods" or "People" or both.

When the brainstormers are finished, they typically use a consensus technique to determine the root cause of the problem. They may decide to measure a particular aspect of the process. In any case, they will have a pretty good idea where the cause of the problem lies. (More informa-

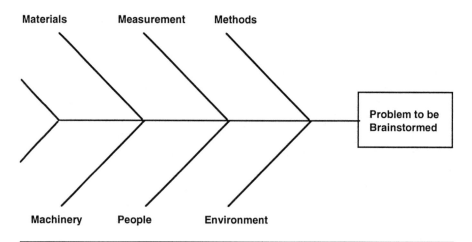

Figure 7.5 Sample Fishbone Diagram

tion on fishbone diagrams and other SPC tools can be found in a number of books on SPC.)

The cause of the nonconformance may turn out to be simple, and therefore the solution will be simple. If the person charged with reviewing and signing the documents did not do so because he was too busy, because he forgot, or because the documents contained "the same things they always contain" and he did not see the point in reviewing them, a direct memo from the CEO—or a "heart-to-heart" chat—may suffice. Other causes will require more in-depth action. If the documents were not reviewed because company procedures require that they be reviewed by a certain person and she happened to be out of the office, then the company procedure should be amended to require (and allow) that the reviewer designate a successor when she is unavailable. If they weren't reviewed because they were revisions and time was short, the company should amend its procedure to allow for such emergency situations.

Some problems may result because a company is too ambitious. For example, one company stated in its procedure on test equipment that all such equipment would be calibrated once a month. When the auditor found that calibrations were not carried out with that frequency, he gave the company a nonconformance. In that case, the company should examine the procedure to see if it is realistic and necessary to call for calibrations to be done so frequently. The once-a-month clause may have been put in the procedure because someone thought "it makes us sound good." If, upon analysis, the company finds that calibrations are needed only once every three months or that quality department personnel can only get to each piece of equipment every two months, the procedure should be changed. If the company finds that calibrations do need to be done once a month, it should give the calibration team the support necessary to meet the schedule.

Implementing Solutions

Once a company has determined the cause of a particular problem, it should perform an internal benchmark, that is, search the entire operation to see if there are other instances of the same problem and what has been done to solve those occurrences. The next step is to plan and implement a solution. The ISO steering committee should work with the heads of the departments affected to come up with a workable solution and then put it into place.

Depending on the problems and their causes, the solutions will range from the simple (collecting all out-of-date documents and issuing current ones) to the complex (writing new procedures and work instructions that comply with the intent of the standards and then training employees in them).

Think About It...

Your company probably has at least one area that would receive a nonconformance during an ISO audit. What corrective action would you prescribe for it? How would you go about implementing the corrective action?

Closeout Actions

Once a company has decided upon a plan for remedying the nonconformances cited by the auditor, it should send a response to the auditor detailing the corrective action. This response should list the nonconformances cited and for each one should do the following:

1. State that the nonconformance will be corrected or justify inaction by explaining how it can be accepted without compromising quality (for example, the item involved is subject to later actions [e.g., inspections] that will uncover and eliminate the problem, or specific training on the procedure will be provided).
2. Show that the company has searched for and corrected all similar problems that the auditor may have missed.
3. Describe the conditions or situations that caused the nonconformance. (The company should not try to say that the nonconformance was an isolated incident or the result of one individual's actions unless it has overwhelming evidence to prove those statements.)
4. Describe the actions that have been or will be implemented to prevent the nonconformance from recurring. (Telling individuals to "pay more attention" is not a sufficient response.)
5. If the implementation of final corrective action will take considerable time, describe the temporary measures that have been or will be implemented to ensure that the nonconformance does not affect quality as it relates to the customer.

The Auditor's Response

When the auditor receives the report of corrective action from the company, he or she will assess the corrective actions taken or planned by the company. The auditor will judge their individual effectiveness and determine if each corrective action is sufficient to eliminate the nonconformance, to ensure a consistent level of quality, and to meet the intent of the standard. If the auditor deems that any or all of the corrective actions are not sufficient, he or she will tell the company that more work is needed. If the auditor deems them to be sufficient, he or she has three options:

1. The auditor can accept the corrective actions and can close the nonconformances. (The auditor will then submit his or her report for review so that ISO registration can be granted. This is most common.)

2. The auditor can request that the company submit evidence that the corrective actions are in place and are working. This evidence may be copies of new policies, procedures, or work instructions; proof of compliance might include, for example, completed calibration forms or samples of products or documents that have been subjected to the corrective actions. (If, upon examination of the evidence, the corrective actions seem sufficient, the auditor will then submit his or her report for review so that ISO registration can be granted.)

3. The auditor can require a reaudit of the affected area(s). (If the company passes this reaudit, the auditor will then submit his or her report for review so that ISO registration can be granted.)

Once registration has been granted, a company should keep all documentation related to the audit (the report, checklists, corrective action reports, lists of corrective actions taken, the auditor's confirmation that corrective action has been effectively implemented, meeting minutes, etc.) on file at least until the next total quality system audit, usually for a period of three years.

Surveillance Visits

Registration is not the end of the ISO process. A company must continue all ISO-related activities because the auditors will conduct periodic follow-up visits every three to six months to monitor the continued effective operation of the quality system. Most auditing firms will schedule periodic visits to a company to assure continued compliance with the standards. Other auditing firms will schedule "surprise" visits for which a company will have little time to prepare. Both types of surveillance visits have the same purpose—to assure that the company maintains its focus on meeting the intent of the standards.

It is vital to remember that continuous adherence to the standards is an accepted part of the registration process. If the auditor notices exceptional nonconformance or a blatant disregard of the company's quality system during a surveillance visit, a company's registration can be withdrawn. While this rarely happens, companies must be aware that it can happen, particularly if the auditor suspects that a company's quality system was implemented only for the ISO audit and was then ignored. For most companies, the surveillance visits simply provide the auditor with additional data that the company continues to comply with the intent of the standard.

Recap

The audit is the culmination of the ISO process. It is a complex action that includes several phases: preparation, the pre-audit, the pre-assessment meeting, sampling, interviewing, observation, tracing, a final report, and corrective action. The audit process is, ideally, a cooperative effort. A company needs to work with the audit team prior to, during, and after the audit itself. A company must be sure that all processes are operational and effective before the audit. ISO audits require records documenting the effectiveness of the quality system. After the audit, a company must take corrective action to remedy any nonconformances recorded during the audit.

Chapter 8

Summary

In the ten years since its inception, the ISO 9000 series of standards has become the most influential set of quality requirements ever, with over 130,000 companies worldwide having achieved certification. The recently introduced QS-9000 series, a combination of ISO 9000 and the quality requirements of Ford, General Motors, and Chrysler, is impacting another 50,000 companies with its mandate for registration or compliance.

Underlying both ISO 9000 and QS-9000 is the requirement for management responsibility, including management review of the system—a responsibility that cannot be delegated. ISO 9000, while maintaining inspection requirements as one avenue to assure the quality of product, also stresses quality by process, that is, quality built into the system.

A quick perusal of the requirements of both ISO and QS-9000 reveals that the traditional areas of focus for a quality standard—areas such as process control, inspection and testing, and control of inspection, measuring, and test equipment—are supplemented by requirements in contract review, purchasing, training, and statistical techniques. It is these types of requirements that truly distinguish ISO from other standards. Neither ISO nor QS-9000 should be seen as a static standard. In fact, the dynamic nature of ISO, the updating of the standard every five years and the inclusion of surveillance audits in the registration process, assures that registered companies will continually improve the quality systems they have implemented.

The ISO 9000 series is not, of course, without its critics—those who argue that it is not sophisticated enough to ensure true quality to the customer, but is simply a predictable level of service or product quality. While it is true that standards such as ISO always lag the best industry practices, full implementation of an ISO-based system should guarantee higher levels of product and service quality to the customer simply through the management review process. If scrap is not being reduced, if customer complaints are not falling, if on-time delivery is not being increased, it is not so much the fault of the standard but of its implementation.

QS-9000 was careful to include more of the requirements of continuous quality improvement into its requirements. The ISO 9000 series is moving more in that direction with expanded requirements in areas such as document *and data* control and corrective *and preventive* action, as well as statistical techniques.

The focus of this book is on helping a company prepare for and pass the registration or compliance audit. The process begins with planning the implementation. The planning phase itself often begins with a presentation to management of the basic requirements of ISO or QS-9000 by a consultant or a knowledgeable employee. This is followed by a process analysis (what is currently in place versus what is required by the standard) and the appointment of an ISO champion.

While the management representative for ISO must be a member of the management team, the actual implementation of the system may be carried out by a direct report of the management representative who does not have full-time management responsibilities. If this is done, the responsibility for continuous review of the system must be maintained by senior management.

Once the process analysis is completed, a small cadre of employees is often trained in the strategies for implementation. This group will often lead the efforts in their departments, will likely help write the procedures that need to be written, and may eventually become part of the internal audit process (all of this depends on the size of a company).

The next step is to write the Tier I policy manual. In this manual, the company commits to comply with each of the 20 elements of ISO or with the requirements of QS-9000. If a policy manual is already in place, it may need to be revised to ensure that all the requirements of ISO and QS are addressed. It is not unusual to complete a milestone chart for registration at this point and to include a failure modes and effects analysis of what can go wrong in the process. This is also a good opportunity to determine which measurements are appropriate to provide the company with data regarding the success of the ISO or QS-9000 implementation process. A company may want to look at rework, design changes, customer complaints, or other measurements to demonstrate a return on the ISO/QS investment.

About four to six months into the process, a company should identify and interview potential registrars. A company may want to check with customers to see who they would recommend and might want to determine where a registrar's mark is held and the value of that mark in countries where the company is or will shortly be doing business. The explosion of the number of registrars in the United States suggests that a company should be very thorough in selecting the potential registrar.

It is critical for any company seeking to achieve QS-9000 registration to understand that not all ISO registrars (or auditors) are qualified to register (or audit to) QS-9000.

Once the plan is in place, a company moves to the implementation phase. This phase often begins with a review of the requirements by each department in terms of specific procedures that need to be created in order to meet the requirements. While the discrepancy analysis conducted at the beginning of the process will likely have provided an overview of these needs, the departmental review conducted in this step is a much more detailed analysis of the difference between requirements and current procedures—perhaps in terms of the quality records that support the implementation of the procedures.

There is also a difference, of course, between having procedures and having fully implemented procedures. Full implementation may require update and revision, additional training, or additional documentation.

Once all the quality system procedures and work instructions are in place, all employees must be trained in the quality system, in those procedures that apply to their jobs, to the overall flow of the improvement cycle (e.g., how management review is conducted, how corrective action is taken, how internal audits are performed), and key elements of the quality system that every employee should know and understand (for example, the company's quality mission statement.)

Once the system is fully implemented, the next step is the internal audit. Typically, at least three months should pass between full implementation and the initial internal audit. Without some passage of time, there is no opportunity to develop the quality records and other documentation that demonstrate compliance. The internal audit, and particularly the checklists used, are a critical element in preparing a company to successfully pass the registration audit.

During the implementation of the system, including training the employees, the ISO/QS-9000 registrar should have been selected and a date set for the pre-audit. Setting the date for the pre-audit helps to keep a company on schedule. The pre-audit should be held about two months after the first cycle of internal audits is completed. This allows sufficient time for the nonconformances noted during the internal audit to have been closed out and some documentation collected as to the effectiveness of those corrective actions.

Audit preparation is one step that many companies overlook for fear that they may somehow be biasing the results of the audit. Experience has shown, however, that companies that thoroughly prepare their employees to honestly and forthrightly deal with auditors generally do better in the audit than those that do not.

The registration audit is, of course, the culminating activity for the process. Depending on the size of a company or facility, audits can range from one day to two weeks in terms of auditor days on-site. If a company has followed the guidelines, has ensured that its system is compliant with the requirements of the standard, and has fully implemented the system, including following up on the nonconformances found by the auditors during the pre-audit, then registration is often achieved during the first registration audit (although written documentation required of systemic improvement may be required).

Remember that neither the ISO 9000 nor the QS-9000 process ends with the registration audit. Both of these systems require surveillance or periodic audits. These are typically scheduled every six months, with a second full audit often scheduled about three months after the initial audit. Auditors expect to see the quality system mature as the process continues, and surveillance audits often look at specific requirements in even more depth than the initial audit.

Today, there is no doubt that the ISO/QS process is continuing to gain momentum. Approved vendor lists for ISO-registered companies are more and more frequently requiring registration to or at least evidence of compliance with the requirements of the standard. Is this the real payoff? There is no doubt that it is part of the payoff, but the real value of registration should be found in the reduction in internal costs and the improved customer satisfaction that comes from fully implementing a company's quality system.

Bibliography

Arter, Dennis R. *Quality Audits for Improved Performance* (1989)
  A good primer on the general concepts and conducts of quality audits. Not ISO specific, but much of the information is similar.

Bureau of Business Practice. *ISO 9000: Handbook of Quality Standards and Compliance* (1992)
  A compilation of information on ISO 9000 and the principles of total quality management and how the two relate.

CEEM Information Systems. *Quality Systems Update* (June 1992–August 1996)
  Monthly newsletter with the most up-to-date information on ISO 9000 regulations, interpretations, registrar information, and trends.

Clements, Richard, Stanley Sidor and Rand Winters, Jr. *Preparing Your Company for QS-90000,* 2nd edition (1996)
  Helpful source for introductory information on QS-9000.

International Organization for Standardization. *ISO 9000 Compendium*
  The ISO 9000 standards themselves.

Lamprecht, James. *ISO 9000: Preparing for Registration* (1992)
  A compilation of information, including case studies.

Peach, Robert W., Editor. *The ISO 9000 Handbook* (1992)
  A compilation of all information available (as of publication date) on ISO 9000, both theory and practice, in the United States and internationally.

Quality System Assessment (QSA), August 1994
  Essential document for QS-9000 audit preparation.

Quality System Requirements – QS-9000, August 1994
  The QS-9000 document itself; over 90 pages.

Index

A

Accreditation, of audit, 118
AENOR, 96
AIAG, see Automotive Industry Action Group
American Bureau of Shipping, 96
American Society for Quality Control, 29
Audit, see also specific types
  approach, 118
  checklist used in, 126, 127
  compliance, 22
  criteria for passing, 97
  determination, 17
  documented, 20
  first-party, 17
  independence of person conducting, 87
  initial meeting, 136
  internal, 17
  manner conducted, 164
  members, independence of, 124
  preparation quiz, 158–159
  process
    auditor friendly, 51
    evolution of, 13
  report, 123
  schedule, 121, 122
  second-party, 18
  surveillance, 22, 90, 97
  team, support needed by, 164
  ten hints for employees in preparing for, 160
  third-party, 14, 18
  what they are not, 21
Auditor(s)
  giving too much information to, 176
  independence of, 19
  lead, 117, 146, 148
  mark, 97
  taking notes by, 143
Automotive Industry Action Group (AIAG), 30

B

Benchmarking, 61, 62, 83
Body language, 143
British Standards Institute (BSi), 95
BS 5750, 16, 26
BSi, see British Standards Institute

C

CASE, see Conformity Assessment Systems Evaluation
CEO involvement, 46
10CFR50, Nuclear Regulatory Commission's, 16
Checklist
  contents of, 132
  internal, 157
  organizing, 131
  reliance of auditors on, 19, 20
  used in audit, 126, 127
Chrysler, 32

197

Confidence factor, 139
Conformity Assessment Systems Evaluation (CASE), 96
Continuous quality improvement (CQI), 27, 28
Contract Review, 169
Control of Nonconforming Product, 170
Control system, features of, 134
Corrective and Preventive Action, 171
Cost
  of audit, 118
  reassessment, 114
CQI, see Continuous quality improvement
Customer preference, of audit, 118
Customer-Supplied Product, 170

D

Deming, W. Edwards, 26, 27
Designated writer, 79
Design Control, 169
Document control system, 80
Document and Data Control, 169
Documentation, 70
Documentation system, 70

E

EC, see European Community
Employees
  hints for, in preparing for audit, 160
  preparing, for interviews, 174–175
European Community (EC), 95

F

Failure modes and effects analysis (FMEAs), 35, 82
Final report, 185
First-party audits, 17
Fishbone analysis, 186
FMEAs, see Failure modes and effects analysis
Ford, 32

G

General Quality Standard, 28
GM, 32

H

Halo effect, 21, 145
Handling, Storage, Packaging and Delivery, 171

I

IMTE, see Inspection, Measuring, and Test Equipment
Inspection, Measuring, and Test Equipment (IMTE), 10, 129, 153, 170
Inspection and Testing, 170
Inspection and Test Status, 170
Institute for Quality Assurance, 116
Internal audit, 17, 119–150
  corroboration and conclusions, 145–146
  final meeting, 146–148
  final report, 148–150
  goals of, 137
  initial meeting, 135–137
    audit schedule, 135–136
    establishment of positive tone, 136–137
  performing, 137–144
    interviewing, 141–144
    observing, 137–138
    sampling, 138–140
    tracing, 140–141
  planning, 120–126
    establishing audit schedule, 121–122
    QS-9000 and internal audit process, 125–126
    selecting auditing team, 122–125
  preparing for, 126–135
    contents of checklist, 132–135
    creation of checklist for audit, 130–132
    identification of performance standards, 129–130

purpose of audit, 128–129
review of systems to be audited, 130
scope of audit, 129
process, 127–128
Internal checklist, 157
Internal Quality Audits, 171
International Organization for Standardization, 5, 94
International Register of Certified Auditors, 115
Interviewing, gathering evidence by, 172, 174–177
IRQA, lead auditor approved by, 124
ISO 8402-1994, 16
ISO 9000
  comprehensive system, 4
  development, 6
  good business practices, 27–28
  history, 5
  minimum requirements, 27
  service industry, 15
ISO auditor, certified, 116
ISO phenomenon, 1–23
  audit process, 16–22
    definition, 17
    documented activities, 20
    evaluation and verification, 21
    independent activities, 17–19
    objective evidence, 20–21
    systematic, 19–20
    what audit is not, 21–22
  evolution of audit process, 13–15
  history of ISO 9000, 5–7
    development of standards, 6–7
    International Organization for Standardization, 5–6
  ISO 9000, 4–5
    comprehensive, 4
    system, 4–5
  ISO 9000 requirements, 7–13
    ISO 9001, 7–12
    ISO 9002, 12
    ISO 9003, 12–13
    ISO 9004, 13
  purpose of audit, 22–23
  service industry, 15–16

ISO/QS-9000 audit, planning implementation, 43–63
  deciding upon registration, 58–62
    benchmark companies, 61–62
    multisite registration, 59–61
  initial preparation, 45–58
    creation of ISO/QS-9000 steering committee, 50–52
    executive endorsement, 46–47
    ISO/QS-9000 champion, 47–48
    ISO/QS facilitators, 52
    ISO/QS-9000 process analysis, 48–50
    presentation of process report to senior leadership, 50
    quality policy manual, 52–53
    step-by-step plan, 53–58
ISO/QS-9000 audit, putting plan into action, 65–92
  contents of quality manual, 70–81
    document and data control, 80–81
    QS-9000 policy manual, 74
    quality policy manual, 71–74
    quality records, 77–78
    standard operating procedures and job work instructions, 74–77
    writing of quality manual, 78–80
  creating quality manual and documentation system, 66–70
    defining quality system, 66–68
    functions altered to meet intent of standard, 68–70
  pre-audit, 89
  registration audit, 89–91
    further action, 90–91
    mining ISO/QS-9000 gold, 91
    possible results, 90
    registration visit, 90
  standardizing and writing SOPs and JWIs, 82–89
    follow-up activities, 88–89
    internal audit guidelines, 86–87
    internal audit process, 85–86
    internal audits, 86
    internal audits for QS-9000, 88
    internal benchmarking, 83

prioritization of functions for standardization, 82
training, 83–85
ISO/QS-9000 champion, qualifications of, 49
ISO/QS implementation, suggested training, 57–58
ISO/QS registration, 185
ISO/quality training, 84
ISO registration, 25
ISO requirements
  contract review, 8
  control of customer-supplied product, 9
  control of inspection, measuring, and test equipment, 10
  control of nonconforming product, 10
  control of quality records, 11
  corrective and preventive action, 11
  design control, 9
  document and data control, 9
  handling, storage, packaging, preservation, and delivery, 11
  inspection and testing, 10
  inspection and test status, 10
  internal quality audits, 11
  management responsibility, 8
  process control 10
  product identification and traceability, 9
  purchasing, 9
  quality system, 8
  servicing, 12
  statistical techniques, 12
  training, 11
ISO steering committee, 185, 187

J

Job work instructions (JWIs), 47, 48, 74–75
Juran, Joseph, 26
JWIs, see Job work instructions

L

Lead auditor, 117, 123, 124, 146, 148
Leading questions, auditor and, 143
Lloyd's Register Quality Assurance Ltd. (LRQA), 100
LRQA, see Lloyd's Register Quality Assurance Ltd.

M

Maintenance schedule, 121
Major nonconformance, 109, 168, 178–180
Malcolm Baldrige National Quality Award, 16, 26
Management Responsibility, 153, 168, 169
Memorandum of understanding (MoU), 95, 100, 110
MIL-Q-9858A, 16
Minor nonconformance, 109, 180
MIS, 68
MoU, see Memorandum of understanding
Multiple sites, company with, 114
Multisite registration, 59

N

NCR, see Nonconformance report
Nonconformance(s), 108–110, 147, 164
  evidence of, 177
  major, 109, 168, 178–180
  minor, 109, 180
  report (NCR), 178
  root cause of, 176
NQA-1, 16
NQAP1, 16
Nuclear Regulatory Commision, 16

O

Objective evidence, 20
Observing, by auditor to gather evidence, 137–138, 141–144

P

PFD, see Process flow diagram
Potemkin Village, of procedures, 152
PPAP, see Production Part Approval Process
Process Control, 170
Process flow diagram (PFD), 79, 141
Product Identification and Traceability, 170
Production Part Approval Process (PPAP), 32, 33
Production schedule, 121
Purchasing, 76, 170
    department, compliance with ISO standards by, 68
    manager, 88

Q

Q-1, 28
QE, see Quality evaluation
QOS, see Quality Operating System
QS-9000
    approved registrars, list of, 35–38
    audit, preparing for, 40
    checklists, 39
    clauses from management responsibility
        management review, 40
        organization, 40
        quality policy, 40
    comparing ISO 9000 and total quality management
        good business practices, 27–28
        ISO as minimum requirements, 27
    enter, 25–41
        checklist for QS-9000 audit, 39–40
        comparing ISO 9000 and total quality management, 26–28
        integrating ISO and CQI, 30
        organization of QS-9000, 30–33
        preparing for QS-9000 audit, 40–41
        QSA, 33–39
        quality requirements of Big Three, 28–30
        sanctioned interpretations, 33

harmonization, 29
history, 29
internalization, 29
mandatory requirements, 39
organization, 30
    appendices, 31
    customer specific requirements, 31, 32
    sector specific requirements, 31, 32
    registration, 31
QSA, see Quality System Assessment
Quality
    evaluation (QE), 100
    mission statement, 71
    Operating System (QOS), 30
    policy, 52, 72–73
    records, 87, 171
    standards, adaptation of worldwide, 3
    system, 169
        Registrars, 96
Quality System Assessment, 32, 33, 39, 41, 120, 125
Quality Systems Update, 33

R

RAB, see Registrar Accreditation Board
Random samples, 140
Reassessment cost, 114
Registrar(s), 45
    Accreditation Board (RAB), 96, 115, 124
    scope, 97
    supplier registered by same, 112
Registration audit, 165–181
    auditor friendly, 152–161
        documentation system, 153–156
        final preparations, 161
        pre-audit, 157–161
        preparation of employees, 156–157
    closeout actions, 188–190
        auditor's response, 189
        surveillance visits, 189–190
    conducting audit, 168–172
    corrective action, 185–188

corroborating, 177
details about audit, 163–165
establishment of relationship, 165
gathering evidence, 172
interviewing, 174–177
implementing solutions, 187–188
nonconformances, 178–181
root cause of problems, 185–187
sampling, 172–174
sharing information, 177
visit with CEO, 168
final meeting, 182–184
final report, 184–185
pre-audit meeting, 162–165
results
   fail, 90
   pass, 90
   provisional, 90
Registration firm, selecting, 93–118
   auditor qualifications, 115–118
     auditor certification, 115–116
     lead auditor skills, 116–118
   confusion over registration, 94–96
     U.S. picture, 95–96
     world picture, 94–95
   criteria for selecting a registrar 96–115
     accreditation, 110–111
     approach, 108–110
     cost, 113–115
     customer preference, 111–113
     scope, 100–108
Reporting phase, after auditing, 146
RvA, 111

S

Sales, 69, 88
Sample(s)
   gathering evidence with, 172–174
   random, 140
   size of, 139
Sanctioned interpretations, 33
Scope

of audit, 118
individual auditor, 107
Second-party audits, 18
Servicing, 171
Shalls, 53
SOPs, see Standard operating procedures
SPC, see Statistical process control
Standard operating procedures (SOPs), 47, 48, 74
Statistical process control (SPC), 186
Statistical Techniques, 171
Supplier Quality Assurance, 28
Surveillance audits, 22, 90, 97

T

Targets for Excellence, 28
Third-party audits, 14, 18
Tier 1, 70
Tier 2, 70
Tier 3, 70
Total quality management (TQM), 25
TQM, see Total quality management
Tracing, gathering evidence by, 137, 140–141, 172
Training, 171
   ISO/quality, 84
   new style of, 84
   roles of in ISO process, 51
Travel time, auditor's, 114

U

UKAS, see United Kingdom Accreditation Service
UL, see Underwriters Laboratories Inc.
Underwriters Laboratories Inc. (UL), 95, 96
United Kingdom Accreditation Service (UKAS), 95, 110, 115

V

Vendor-approval process, 2
Vendors, 69